The Consolations of **Imperfection**

Learning to Appreciate Life's Limitations

DONALD McCULLOUGH

Brazos Press

A Division of Baker Book House Co
Grand Rapids, Michigan 49516

© 2004 by Donald McCullough

Published by Brazos Press
a division of Baker Book House Company
P.O. Box 6287, Grand Rapids, MI 49516-6287
www.brazospress.com

Printed in the United States of America

Library of Congress Cataloging-in-Publication Data
McCullough, Donald W., 1949–
    The consolations of imperfection : learning to appreciate life's limitations / Donald McCullough.
        p.   cm.
    Includes bibliographical references.
    ISBN 1-58743-077-0
    1. Consolation. 2. Imperfection. 3. Loss (Psychology)—Religious aspects—Christianity. 4. Aging—Religious aspects—Christianity. 5. Aging—Psychological aspects. I. Title
    BV4905.3.M347 2004
    248.8′6—dc22   2003018401

Scripture is taken from the New Revised Standard Version of the Bible, copyright 1989 by the Division of Christian Education of the National Council of the Churches of Christ in the USA. Used by permission.

To
Woody and Stephne Garvin,
my faithful friends,
with gratitude and love

Contents

Acknowledgments

I am grateful for the counsel, encouragement, and persistence of literary agents Kathryn Helmers and Chip MacGregor.

I am grateful for the editorial guidance of Rodney Clapp. It has been a delight to work with him and the rest of the team at Brazos Press.

I am especially grateful for my wife, Shari. Her merciful love has made me a better person, even as her merciless honesty has made me a better writer.

1

Colliding with the Inevitable

The Limitations of a Masterpiece

There are limitations in life.

This would seem beyond dispute: our eyes need glasses to read the print in this sentence; our children make choices that sadden us, and we can do nothing about it; our parents die before bestowing the affirmation we crave; our self-images get beat up by an honest inventory of our failures; our marriages suffer disappointments, even dissolution; our dreams of achievement dissipate in the unforgiving daylight of middle age; our friends start showing up in the obituaries, and a little voice whispers that we'll soon be joining them. The list is endless.

But many of us—probably most of us, most of the time—pretend these limitations don't exist. They are uncomfortable, if not excruciatingly painful, so naturally we try to deny them.

A few years ago my mother, my eldest daughter, and I chartered a twenty-eight-foot boat in Seattle. We planned to sail north, up the west side of Whidbey Island to Mutiny Bay. I calculated the trip would take no longer than a day.

Leaving the marina, our boat heeled in a steady wind and pointed into a world of varying blues. Everything was perfect, or so it seemed to me. But as the day wore on, Mom and Jennifer became increasingly silent. They seemed weary, ready to end our adventure. I had neither understanding nor sympathy. How could they not be having fun, with water slapping our hull, a tiller tugging slightly to leeward, the wind blowing in our faces, and a fine film of salt covering our skin? What more could anyone want? As Rat said to Mole, "There is *nothing*—absolutely nothing—half so much worth doing as simply messing about in boats."

They complained that we had been in the same place for a long time.

"It's just an illusion," I assured them. "It just *seems* that we can't get around this end of the island. Look, the wind is blowing hard. We're moving at a good speed. Don't worry. We'll be there before long."

"But Dad," Jennifer said, "I've been watching those trees on the island for a long time, and they haven't moved. We're not going anywhere. I'm worried we won't get to Mutiny Bay before dark."

"Nonsense, Jennifer. I've been sailing a long time, and I know what I'm doing. Get something to eat; you'll feel better."

"I'm not hungry."

Have you ever had an argument in which you became more dogmatic even as you became less certain? That's what happened to me that day. I argued more vehemently as my doubts grew. I didn't want to see the truth of our circumstances. I was practicing selective perception at a championship level. I didn't want to encounter any evidence contrary to my cherished convictions, so I fought hard in a battle I knew I was losing.

Here's a rule of life you can count on: eventually the truth catches up with you. That's the problem with denial; it works only until circumstances overwhelm you. For me, on that day near Whidbey Island, enlightenment came with the fishing boats. I thought we could sail through their lines and nets, and we could have, had we actually been making headway. But because we were drifting, we floated back into their gear and got cussed out in the exquisitely effective manner of angry fishermen. I responded with my own colorful comments about sailboats having the right of way, no doubt muttering something about no-account motorboaters.

When we finally got out of the mess, I went to the cabin to consult my charts. Then it occurred to me: the currents in that part of Puget Sound were especially fierce, and we were attempting to sail against an incoming tide. Our little boat was no match for the power of the Pacific pouring into the bay. My mother and daughter were right. Fortunately, about the time my pride turned to embarrassment, the tide also turned and we made it to our destination as the sun was setting.

Can-Do Culture

Denial works, but only briefly. Eventually the little boat called *Me* will sail into difficulties of some kind, and ignoring them only imperils the journey. Most of us would like to navigate a course toward personal wholeness; most of us would like to fulfill our potential. And we would prefer not to fight against a flood tide. The forces of nature, however, care not a whit about our personal preferences. The only way to reach the west side of Whidbey Island is to reckon with these limitations, to learn how to adapt to their reality.

Unfortunately, our reluctance to do this is supported by a determinedly optimistic culture that runs on a can-do confidence in every individual's ability—given a positive attitude and hard work—to overcome all obstacles on the way to success. This spirit has flourished, in part, because of geography: the seemingly boundless expanse of our continent promised new opportunities, and this promise energized and focused our

13

expectations. In the words of Parker Palmer, "We resist the very ideas of limits, regarding limits of all sorts as temporary and regrettable impositions on our lives. Our national myth is about the endless defiance of limits: opening the western frontier, breaking the speed of sound, dropping people on the moon, discovering 'cyberspace' at the very moment when we have filled old-fashioned space with so much junk that we can barely move. We refuse to take no for an answer."

One reason we refuse to take no for an answer is that we've discovered that a stubbornly positive attitude helps get us through many of life's difficulties. Your body rolls out of bed more easily when you anticipate a productive day; your marriage works better when you congratulate your spouse on the part of the car that is *not* dented; your children will develop better self-images if you affirm rather than nag; you'll adjust better to new circumstances when you imagine the opportunities they provide. Being grateful for what you *do* have is almost always a healthy discipline of the soul.

As a philosophy, "the power of positive thinking" isn't so much wrong as incomplete. It doesn't tell the whole story. What it fails to mention is that some limitations will not allow passage, no matter how firm one's resolve. Sometimes your path is blocked by stone walls, and even if you give yourself a pep talk that would win applause from Tony Robbins or Robert Schuller, and you give yourself plenty of running distance to build up speed, you will never break through them. Your wife leaves you. Your youngest child dies. You face honestly a deep moral flaw in your character. Your boss fires you after twenty of the best years of your life. Under these circumstances, telling yourself to cheer up won't help much. Perhaps a Superman or a Superwoman could push through the wall, but the rest of us had better protect our noses.

Why, then, do we continue to imbibe from the bottle of positive thinking? We've joined the rest of our culture at the Can-Do

14

Cantina and quaff glass after glass, though we know it won't sustain us and we'll pay for it in the morning. Why do we find it so difficult to walk out of the bar?

The real reason we can't quit drinking is that we are afraid. We're doing our best to forget something that terrifies us: we fear *the* limitation, the mother of all limitations, what William James called the "worm at the core" of human pretensions to happiness. What we want to banish from our awareness is death.

As Ernest Becker has shown in his masterful *The Denial of Death*, this fear is embedded in our unconscious minds. Attempts to keep it buried shape our character and influence our behavior far more than we realize, often becoming the hidden cause of anxieties and neuroses and even psychoses. Our "life project," as Becker puts it, consists in learning to cope with this final limitation.

If Becker is correct—and I believe he is—then of course we hate *all* limitations. We hate them, not simply because they're uncomfortable or cause suffering, but because they open a cellar door we would rather keep shut, allowing a dark, frightening shadow to escape and haunt us.

I'm not suggesting that stiff joints in the morning have us planning our own funeral services. It's more subtle than that. Feet that grumble displeasure at being forced out of bed also whisper something to us just below the range of awareness that is easily perceptible by the ears of the unconscious. What they say is this: *This is just the beginning. You're falling apart. It's just a matter of time before nothing works any more.*

We may argue against the facts of our situation, but eventually the truth will have its way with us. No matter how thoroughly we repress fear of death, and no matter how skillfully we ignore the limitations that are its advance warning system, we simply can't get through life without running into some very unforgiving, immovable walls.

15

Owning It All

As someone who has already skinned his nose on plenty of limitations, I've decided to take a careful look at them. Personal integrity, it seems to me, calls for owning the whole of one's experience—the painful as well as the joyous, the shameful as well as the praiseworthy, the shadows as well as the light, the limitations as well as the possibilities. By "owning" I do not mean excusing the bad or pretending it's good; some things *in themselves* are just plain awful, period. They can be neither explained nor justified. But they should be acknowledged and examined and, as far as possible, understood and appreciated. Integrity has to do with integration, holding together in one coherent whole the wide-open spaces and the impassable walls; integrity has to do with allowing everything to fit together and make its own contribution.

A character in one of Walker Percy's novels asks, "Is it possible for people to miss their lives in the same way one misses a plane?" Percy describes such a person: "Not once in his entire life had he allowed himself to come to rest in the quiet center of himself but had forever cast himself forward from some dark past he could not remember to a future that did not exist. Not once had he been present for his life. So his life had passed like a dream."

Well, I don't want to miss my life. I have no interest in casting myself forward to some future that never will exist, even if my fantasies might provide short-term relief for anxiety. I would rather be present for the whole shebang. Now that I'm fifty-three years old, I know I will be forced to encounter more limitations in the not-too-distant future. If possible, I aim to be ready for them. Wayne Gretzky, the greatest hockey player of all time, once said, "I always skate to where the puck is going rather than where it's been." And if the puck is headed for a hulking goalie, that's the direction to skate.

16

Even more, I want to learn to *appreciate* the limitations, to see and affirm the contribution they make to the picture of my life. They may not be good in themselves, but do they, I wonder, serve a good purpose in the creation of me?

The Creator as Artist

Here are my central assumptions: a loving Creator is at work on each of us, and this Creator is a true artist, a maker of masterpieces.

This metaphor invites us to consider what every artist knows: great art is not possible without limitations. Igor Stravinsky has written of the difference between unrestricted freedom, which is an anguish, and creative freedom, which "consists in my moving about within the narrow frame that I have assigned myself for each one of my undertakings. I shall go even farther: my freedom will be so much the greater and more meaningful the more narrowly I limit my field of actions and the more I surround myself with obstacles. Whatever diminishes constraint diminishes strength."

It might help us to think of God using limitations in a similar way. Any metaphor has its own limitations, but if it's a good one, the imaginative space it opens allows us to see things a bit more clearly.

In the past year I've taken up photography. My father gave me his Hasselblad, one of the finest cameras made, and I'm doing my best to be worthy of it: I've been studying the technical manuals and the principles of composition; I've been borrowing books from the library to ponder the masterpieces of Weston and Cunningham and Adams. Then I've traipsed along the beaches and lagoons and hills of San Diego County trying to make negatives that I can turn into interesting black-and-white prints. Except for the two occasions I spent hours composing and snapping pictures, only to discover I had neglected to put film in the camera, it has been fun, and I've had the sense that it's helping one who spends most of his time working with words to find a greater balance by attending to images.

One of the first principles of composition I learned is that I have to limit my view of reality. No photograph can record everything the eye sees, and so a necessary limitation must take place. On the focusing screen of my camera, I can include something as large as a forest or as small as a flower, but I have to make a choice before snapping the shutter; I have to crop my perception of the world around me. Great photographers do this with consummate, awe-inspiring skill. Should the corner of this cloud be included? And what about that branch on the left? And would the rock in the foreground add depth or distraction? Too much will clutter the picture; too little may not tell the story.

Then again, maybe there is no such thing as too little. Edward Weston, during his Carmel years, transformed knots of seaweed and pieces of rock into works of art, enabling the viewer to see things she might otherwise have stepped over, had she been at the beach, without so much as pausing to notice. Less may sometimes be more.

The photographer, whether focusing on an immense mountain or a tiny droplet, must—*must*—set boundaries, commit himself or herself to limitations.

And when a print is made, what do we see within the picture itself, if not a series of limitations? Recall any of your favorite prints by Ansel Adams—*Moonrise*, perhaps, or *El Capitan*, or *Mt. McKinley and Wonder Lake*. Are they not—*essentially*—aesthetically arranged patterns of limitations? Moon and mountain and sky and cloud and lake and tree, white against black and black against white—each thing sharply restricted by the other, each thing finding its identity in its limitation. And Adams, to do more than just record what he saw, to make art, would use a red filter to darken the sky, to make the contrast even greater. Then, in the darkroom, he would expose certain

18

areas of the print more than others—dodging here and burning there—to intensify and dramatize the natural limitations.

So is it possible, do you think, that God is up to something like this with the picture of our lives? The limitations we experience may well serve noble purposes in the creation of you and me. This does not, I hasten to add, clear up the mystery of why God chose to work a particular way; nor does it turn bad things into good things. There are no easy answers to questions that emerge from the confusion and pain of some limitations we endure. But without trying to turn white into black or black into white, it's important to see how the picture may look when we step back from it and view it from a distance.

I've been remembering recently something my father said when he held my daughter in his arms: "Grandchildren are God's compensation for growing old." What brought this to mind was holding my own grandchild, Timothy. Now that I'm undeniably into middle age, I'm more aware than ever of the relentless advance of time. But when I see Timothy's wispy blond hair and his blue eyes and his dimpled cheeks, and I see him look up at me and smile, as if he actually recognizes me and already loves me, I understand what my father meant. The compensation seems more valuable than what I've lost.

So I'm wondering, what are the other compensations of imperfection? Do our limitations offer gifts, if only we have the eyes to see them and the good sense to appreciate them? And do these limitations and their benedictions somehow fit together in a way that makes the picture of our lives a work of art, even a masterpiece?

This is what I want to explore in this book, and I invite you to join me.

2

When Getting Out of Bed Hurts

The Limitations of the Body

Recently, I decided to change dry cleaners. They had once again shrunk my trousers. I have never understood the concept of dry cleaning—how fabric can be cleaned without at least getting damp (I once heard something about chemicals and felt this was one of those things, like sausage, about which one was better off not asking too many questions)—but it seemed obvious that those responsible for this mysterious alchemy needed to adjust the formula and quit breathing the fumes. This was getting annoying, not to mention expensive.

Somehow I managed to fasten the top button and went about my day—a day in which I became aware of something I had not noticed before, something fleshly hanging over my belt on both sides of my body. At odd times, such as when I talked on the telephone or sat at my desk, I found myself fingering the bulge. I squeezed it between thumb and forefinger, taking its measure and telling myself that it was the fault of the idiots who had turned the waist of my trousers into a kidney-crusher and was, in fact, nothing at all to worry about. Nothing at all, no siree, not worth paying any attention to whatsoever.

But doubt kept rising like the effects of bad pastrami, eventually exploding into a belch of disgust. I'm getting fat! How could this happen to me—*me!*—the one who at least once in a while orders a salad instead of a Big Mac, who runs seven miles a day, who prides himself on a lean and mean body, who was not supposed to have to deal with this sort of nonsense?

Then I noticed other things: my "laugh lines" are no longer funny; I have fissures down my cheeks that remind me of crevasses I have seen on Mt. Rainier; I spend more time cutting the hair in my ears than the lawn in my backyard; I now consider it extreme recklessness to pass a restroom without availing myself of the opportunity; I have discovered how economically prudent it is to buy the large box of Imodium; I even think about my prostate and wonder what, exactly, it does for a guy.

This inventory leads me to a startling conclusion: I am my age. Before long I will have to look into insurance for convalescent care and be more polite to cemetery plot salesmen. I should have foreseen trouble when, three years ago, I received my first issue of *Modern Maturity*—and actually read it, studying with interest Sophia Loren's age-defying secrets.

No doubt about it, my body is aging, and because I'm neither wine nor cheese, I don't consider this a happy turn of events. I'm sure I'm not alone. The limitations of the body are something most of us ignore until they force their way into our consciousness, and then we do everything we can to jump over or get around or break through them.

Delaying the Inevitable

The first line of defense against an aging body is to pretend it's not happening. According to *Health* magazine, the average age women consider the "end of youth" is fifty-four. Yes, I would agree that fifty-four is the end of youth. As is thirty. But who can fuss with this elastic understanding of the concept? Who wants to lose one's membership in the most prestigious club in our culture?

Even when you get conscripted into that other club and your AARP card shows up in the mail, you think there has been a big mistake because you still *feel* young. One of the major surprises of middle age, if you ask me, is that you don't feel much different on the inside. My body may be fifty-three years old, but my spirit feels about twenty or twenty-five. I had always imagined a fifty-three-year-old would feel . . . well, fifty-three. Mature, wise, responsible. I never would have guessed that someone my age could still feel an overpowering urge to flip a spoonful of peas across the dining room, or want to drive eighty miles per hour with all the windows down and rock-n-roll blasting from the stereo, or, for that matter, still think about sex. A cruel reality of aging is that the body generally falls apart before the spirit. So I can understand the women who think youth does not end until fifty-four.

When denial no longer works, some people resort to more drastic measures to forestall the signs of aging. Wonderbras and buttboosters and control-top pantyhose can only do so much, and certain parts of the body beg for cutting or stretching or vacuuming or tucking. Now that baby boomers are crossing the fifty-year mark, the number of elective surgeries to reshape the body is soaring faster than breasts and bottoms are sagging. According to the American Society of Plastic Surgeons, the number of people choosing cosmetic surgery in 2001 was 7.5 million, three times the number in 1992. The most popular procedures were nose reshaping, liposuction, eyelid surgery, breast augmentation, and facelift. And if you prefer nonsurgical assistance with your appearance, you can have chemical peels, Botox and collagen injections, and laser hair removals. "Makeovers," Douglas Coupland said, "are *the* official art form of the 1990s, you know." What would he say about the first decade of the twenty-first century?

A recent article in the *AARP Bulletin* says, "No one knows how many Americans buy remedies like 'youth' hormone treatments, megavitamin cocktails, herbal elixirs and the like. But experts say it's a multibillion dollar industry that's exploding. Longevity clinics, some charging $2,000 a visit, are popping up all around the country. Anti-aging entrepreneurs also hawk their wares on television infomercials, in direct mail solicitations and on more than a thousand websites."

But strategies of denial are, at best, only ways of delaying the inevitable. You can exercise until you have buns of steel, eat nothing but tofu and sprouts, drink carrot juice and pop vitamin pills, lather your skin with rich moisturizers and alpha hydroxy acid, suck the fat and stretch the sag, never so much as even *think* about chocolate cheesecake—you can be perfectly righteous in bodily ministrations—and still you cannot avoid bodily limitations. Simply put, your body will wear out. Taking care of yourself, with plenty of exercise and a proper diet, will certainly offer rewards; very likely, it will enhance your health and maybe even add years to your life. Sooner or later, though, things will deteriorate.

The body is so vulnerable! A microscopic virus can send you to bed with a cold or to the hospital with HIV; an unseen crack in the sidewalk can leave you wrapped in plaster and hobbling on crutches; a little stone, no bigger that a tiny grain of sand, can slide down your urethra, causing you to beg for a shot of morphine. And all these ailments bring with them something more than pain: they remind you of the approaching Limitation on the final side of all limitations; they remind you of death.

Freedom from a Futile Fight

Believe it or not, there are consolations in all this. The limitations of the body offer graces worthy of contemplation and gratitude.

When we accept the limitations of the body, we can be set free from a futile fight. To be disciplined in exercise, to eat nutritional food, to get enough sleep, to use sunscreen—to be a good steward of the body—are worthy practices, and they may protect us from disease and maximize energy and prolong life. But these things can become tyrants holding merciless sway over our lives. Jacques Ellul, the French lawyer-theologian, once said that the means one uses to achieve desired ends will always overwhelm those ends; a means which aims toward a goal will accumulate power and respect and, before long, will become more important than the end for which it was created. We've all seen this principle at work. Create an agency to eradicate poverty, say, or to accomplish some other good, and before long the agency becomes a bureaucracy with its own life, an entity that develops its own constituents and culture; the means have become the end.

This happens, too, in the maintenance of health. A program of exercise or nutrition can become an end in itself, undermining the very thing it seeks to achieve. Last week, on the evening news, I watched a report about a man who is convinced that a drastically reduced intake of calories will prolong human life. So he gets up at 4:00 A.M. every day to wash his vegetables, a big job because he eats nothing but salad. The video clip showed him sitting at the dinner table with his family; as they ate a normal meal, he munched away on his lettuce, resolutely continuing a quest for perfect health that has taken him from thin to skinny. I tried to imagine how he must feel—cold, hungry, tired—and I wondered why, in that condition, he would want to live extra years. He even admitted his sex life has suffered.

24

"But," he cheerfully said, "when your libido drops, you really don't miss it all that much." Perhaps that's one of the consolations of imperfection, but it's definitely not one I had in mind when I started this book. If you extend his reasoning to its logical conclusion, you could say that when everything shuts down and you're lying in the grave, it will be all right because you really won't miss anything. Which raises the question, why bother? His means, it seems to me, have overtaken the end.

Many years ago, when I first started running, I read a book by a world-famous marathoner. He witnessed to the cardiovascular benefits of this exercise, and he offered tips on clothing and weekly routines and diet. Then, as an aside, he mentioned how every Friday evening he enjoys a big cigar. I was scandalized! How could someone who punished his body with twenty-mile runs indulge himself with this dangerous pleasure? He explained that it was important to remember that the point of good health is to enjoy life; we should run to live, he said, not live to run. Although I've long forgotten his tips about running, I've remembered his cigar. It's a reminder to keep things in perspective. Exercise and other healthy habits are not themselves the goal; at best, they are means leading to the very limited end of good health, an end that will itself come to an end. Every body, no matter how buff and beautiful, will age and die. Looking this inevitability straight in the eye without blinking, and accepting its truth *for me*, can liberate from a compulsive quest for the unattainable.

If we see ourselves in a battle against aging, we will be condemned to a stressful existence of dodging the enemy's bullets and nursing our wounds and planning new strategies to stay in the fight. That would be hard enough, but adding to our troubles is the certainty that we will lose, and thus every aching muscle and deepening wrinkle mocks us and cracks the whip over us, forcing us either to work harder or to raise the white flag as we grab the potato chips and head for the couch. Ironically, this stress undermines the very health we seek.

25

Perhaps we would be better off changing the image from warfare to stewardship. Rather than seeing ourselves in a losing fight, we might do well to imagine ourselves on a journey that takes us through different stages. At each stage our bodies will encounter new limitations, and rather than fight against them, perhaps we should surround them and integrate them into our lives in a way that maximizes strength and energy. Our challenge is not to waste energy on the unattainable but to be good stewards of the manageable. Do my knees hurt when I stumble out of bed and walk down the hallway to fire up the coffee pot? Rather than battling this pain as an enemy to be defeated, which may cause me to ignore the pain and run harder than ever in an effort to conquer it, until my knees completely give out, it would be better to say to myself, "This is normal for fifty-three-year-old knees. Now what do I do? Should I cut back on my mileage? Should I schedule more days of rest? Should I try another sort of exercise that involves less pounding on pavement?" This limitation, in other words, becomes part of me, not an external foe, and I do my best to incorporate it into my life in a way that honors both my need for exercise and the realities of aging. I will be relieved of the anxiety of fighting a losing battle, and the consequent peace I gain will contribute to my overall health.

More than Your Body

Another gift bestowed by physical limitations is the reminder that we are more than our bodies. This is easy to forget, living as we do in a culture that worships at the altar of Body Beautiful. All day long, from radio and TV and magazines and the Internet, the priests of this religion preach the blessedness of lotions and ab-rollers and clothing and colognes and jewelry, mediating a way of salvation from wretched aging to Eternal Youth. One begins to believe, as a tenet of unquestioned dogma,

26

that human beings *are* their bodies, no more and no less, and that one's worth is exactly proportional to one's sex appeal. "To lose confidence in one's body," Simone de Beauvior said, "is to lose confidence in oneself."

But this attitude is terribly mistaken. Simply put, if you expect your body to provide self-worth and security, you want more than it can give; any image you can groom into being cannot define your personal identity. You are more than your body. You are spirit, too, and that spiritual dimension exists in relationships—with God and other people and maybe even your dog, who doesn't give a flying milk-bone what you look like.

The limitations of the body serve as a reminder of this. The very rebellion we feel against them, the part of us that fights every sign of aging, flows from a spirit that knows there has to be something more, a spirit that strives relentlessly toward something beyond the body, even if it can't exactly name what that something is. Our unhappiness about new wrinkles or lost hair, or our outrage at disease or injury, is a voice shouting, "I am more than this!"

When Christopher Reeve fell from a horse and injured his spine, he did not surrender to his paralysis, allowing it to define him, but fought back with incredible courage. He become a larger man, working not only for his own recovery but also for increased research on the problem of spinal cord injuries. And as Michael J. Fox now contends with Parkinson's Disease, an important change is happening in his life, a change for the better. "The ten years since my diagnosis," he wrote in his memoir, "have been the best ten years of my life, and I consider myself a lucky man." The limitations of the body have not limited these men, because they are much more than their bodies. Their afflictions have released an inner beauty and a force that will not be kept down by malfunctioning nerves and muscles.

I do not mean to diminish the suffering of Christopher Reeve or Michael J. Fox or others in similar situations; I do not mean

27

to chirp a cheery "every cloud has a silver lining," and thus make light of the crushing burdens borne by many people. At the age of forty-nine, Andre Dubus stopped to help some disabled motorists and was struck by an oncoming car that sentenced him to a wheelchair for the rest of his life. Dubus issued a warning against mindless optimism when he wrote, "To view human suffering as an abstraction, as a statement about how plucky we all are, is to blow air through brass while the boys and girls march in parade off to war."

What he says is true. Yet, with a circumspection befitting one in good health, I must add that when I read his short stories and essays and hear not only his anguished cry over not being able to run again or how difficult it is to get through his daily routines, but also hear him speak of receiving Holy Communion or flirting with a beautiful young woman in a miniskirt, tears fill my eyes, partly in astonishment at his prose and partly because he touches my own crippled heart. Reflecting on that woman in the miniskirt, he wrote,

> Living in the world a cripple allows you to see more clearly the crippled hearts of some people whose bodies are whole and sound. All of us, from time to time, suffer this crippling. . . . Yet in a city whose very sidewalks show the failure of love . . . a young woman turned to me with instinctive anger or pride, and seeing me in a wheelchair she at once felt not pity but lighthearted compassion. For seeing one of her own kind wounded, she lay down the shield and sword she had learned to carry . . . and with the light of sun between us, ten or fifteen feet between us, her face and voice embraced me.

When you read lines like these you know you're in the presence of someone who is so much more than his broken body, someone whose very brokenness has become the venue for a display, like fireworks against the night sky, of a transcendent human spirit.

An Opportunity for Growth

The limitations of the body also provide an opportunity for growth. Granted, tuition in this school can seem high for the lessons imparted; even a costly education, though, should be received with gratitude.

A few years ago my father wanted to take a picture of me sailing on San Francisco Bay, and so he positioned himself (comfortably) on the shore, and I cruised back and forth in front of him looking for all the world like I knew what I was doing, and an impressive photograph now hangs in my study to prove it. The picture, though, has more meaning for me than for most viewers, because it was taken just moments before the wind shifted and, without thinking, I reached up to slow the boom as it swung across the boat. Big mistake. The sail on a twenty-seven-foot boat moves with considerable force. The instant I touched it my upper arm snapped in two.

The following weeks were not fun, not at all what I had planned for my summer vacation. I was single at the time, and this right-hander suddenly had to learn how to be a left-hander. I had to manage eating and shaving and tying my shoes and attending to highly personal matters—at first with laughable awkwardness, until gradually I adjusted to the change. I never mastered writing with my left hand, but eventually everything else felt comfortable. Today, I'm not exactly ambidextrous, though almost; my left hand continues to be dominant in many things, such as driving and reaching for things. The immobilization of my right arm caused some sort of rewiring in my brain, with the result that my left hand learned to do things it had never before done.

29

After the paramedics had gotten me off my boat and to the hospital, and after the morphine had altered my view of the situation so that I was cracking jokes like David Letterman on a good night, the emergency room doctor told me I had a fractured humerus. Perhaps I wasn't funny, after all, but I didn't think he needed to add insult to injury. But hey! I was in no mood for a fight. I decided to let it pass and be his best friend. Actually, I was in the mood to befriend the whole world. I wanted to hug little children and shelter the homeless; I was desperate to pass out flowers to strangers while humming Beethoven's "Ode to Joy." So I smiled benevolently when my new best friend announced he was going to put my arm in a brace, though I sobered up enough to ask an important question: "Doctor, will I still be able to run?" He only smiled at me—the sort of smile that says, in a highly professional way, "You stupid, compulsive jerk. I'm not paid enough to work with idiots like you."

When the morphine wore off, the only thing I felt like humming was the funeral dirge. I knew I wouldn't run, not for a long time. After a good deal of moaning and groaning (you would have thought both my legs had been amputated), I decided I would have to be content with walking. Yes, I know: I've read reports claiming this is as good for you as running. Frankly, I'm not convinced. Even if every doctor on the faculty of Harvard Medical School swore this on a stack of Bibles, I wouldn't believe it. I have no scientific evidence for my position, of course, only a runner's arrogance.

When I began to walk, at first I saw only mental images of aluminum walkers and old people shuffling along the manicured paths of a retirement community. Eventually, though, I began to see other things. The slower pace afforded more freedom to look around and notice, for example, trees. I had always been aware of them, in a general sense, as in "tall pointy things," but I had not paid much attention to them. Suddenly I saw the amazing variety in Marin County—palms and redwoods and elms. Actually, I wasn't too sure about the elms, so I bought a book to help me, a field guide to trees. I'm still no botanist, but I know more than before. A broken arm had limited my exercise, and this limitation enabled growth in a different part of my life.

The story of my injury and what I learned from it is like a report from the bench of a minor league team. Others have played in the major leagues; they have endured far worse, and consequently have learned far more. For many years I was a Presbyterian pastor. One of the joys of that position was being invited into the lives of people during times of personal crisis—times that filled me with a sense of inadequacy as I did my best to manifest God's love, often by doing little more than listening and weeping and stammering out some prayers. I've been by the bedside of people afflicted with cancer, multiple sclerosis, Lou Gehrig's disease, heart attacks—you name it. And almost without exception they would say something like this: "Pastor, I hate this situation, and I wouldn't want anyone to go through what I've been through, but I want to tell you something." They would usually pause, not sure how to articulate their feelings. "It's odd . . . I'm not sure I can explain it. Somehow, in the midst of this mess, I've experienced more than the pain. I've learned more about God and other people and myself than I ever thought possible. I've *felt* things that are new to me." By then, emotions had usually lodged in their throats and they would simply squeeze my hand. They had come to a limitation in life, and they had discovered life in the limitation.

31

3

Okay, So I Wasn't a Perfect Parent

The Limitations of Relationships

We cannot live without other people. We cannot live easily with other people. Herein lies much of the difficulty in being human.

We are social animals. A study at Johns Hopkins University, examining the health records of thirteen hundred medical students over a period of eighteen years, revealed that the strongest prognosticator for cancer, mental illness, and suicide was a lack of intimacy with family. Another study of seven thousand people in Alameda, California, revealed that people with few close contacts tended to die two to three times sooner than those who saw their friends regularly—a figure that held up even after adjustments were made for smoking, poor health histories, and other negative factors. We *need* others.

In retreats and workshops I have often illustrated the importance of human community by telling about redwood trees.

Whereas most trees have a root structure that corresponds roughly in size and shape to the pattern of their branches, redwoods have extremely shallow roots. They are able to stay standing, even in severe storms, because their roots intertwine; the trees hold each other, as it were, and create a secure foundation. This is true enough, and a nice image of how we should support and strengthen one another.

But people are more complicated than redwood trees. Sometimes the roots of others are too fragile or rotted to help us; sometimes our own roots are too short to reach those of the nearest tree. Sometimes other trees fall on top of us. We're caught in a paradox: we need other people to keep upright, but those very people make it difficult.

We all want to be loved. Love from others—their loyalty and affection and care and encouragement and passion and longsuffering—makes possible our greatest joys. And we never seem to get enough love. Within each of us is a gnawing hunger for more.

James Baldwin, in one of his books, described this scene:

> The joint, as Fats Waller would have said, was jumping. . . . And during the last set, the saxophone player took off on a terrific solo. He was a kid from some insane place like Jersey City or Syracuse. But somewhere along the line he had discovered he could say it with a saxophone. He stood there, wide-legged, humping the air, filling his barrow chest, shivering in the rags of his twenty-odd years, and screaming through the horn, "Do you love me? Do you love me? Do you love me?" And again, "Do you love me? Do you love me? Do you love me?" The same phrase unbearable, endlessly and variously repeated with all the force the kid had. . . . The question was terrible and real. The boy was blowing with his lungs and guts out of his own short past. . . . The men on the stand stayed with him cool and at a little distance, adding and questioning. . . . But each man knew that the boy was blowing for every one of them.

He was blowing for all of us. And maybe one reason he was playing our song is that, though we long for love, we often feel wounded by the actual love we have received.

Disappointment Runs in the Family

Some years ago, the congregation I was serving asked my father to speak at its annual men's retreat. I was pleased that he accepted the invitation; we lived many miles apart, and the retreat would provide an opportunity to see each other. When the time came for the event, his talks were well received, as I had expected they would be. I was proud of him.

We concluded the retreat with a time in which the men could offer observations about the weekend. One of the first to address the group said, "I thought John did a great job, but to tell the truth, what meant the most to me was watching John and Don relate to each other as father and son. I did not have a good relationship with my father . . ." He choked up and we waited. "Well, anyway," he said, having difficulty getting it out, "I felt blessed to witness the obvious love they have for each other."

His words opened a floodgate: all around the room men stood, waiting their turn to talk. It was a time of honest vulnerability, each expressing some sort of painful, unfinished business with his father. One man said, "My father and I were estranged as long as I can remember. He recently died before we had a chance to become reconciled, and I feel so sorry, so bad." Another said, "I'm a very successful man, a leader in my profession, but I've never once heard my father tell me he was proud of me, and though by now it shouldn't matter, it does, and I realize how much of my life has been spent trying to get that approval." Another said, "I'm always struggling to get my father's approval—and he's been dead ten years!" Yet another said, "I've had a great deal of anger toward my father, and I ask for prayers that I will learn to forgive him." On and on the comments went, my own father and I sitting stunned, not sure what to say, if indeed we needed to say anything. Something important was happening, and we sensed that the tender spirit present was maybe nothing less than God's Spirit.

Not only are children disappointed with their parents, parents are sometimes disappointed with their children. Every parent, it seems, believes his or her child will be the next Einstein or Mozart, and how can that first-grade teacher not see the amazing potential of The Little Wonder? And worse, how can that child, a few years later, choose to travel a different road? How can that daughter turn her back on home and just walk away into a very different lifestyle? How can that son reject his parents' values, the morality he had been lovingly taught, and use his free will in self-destructive ways?

A pastor once told me the worst moment of his life was when he saw his son for what he really was—a drug pusher. "I wanted to grab him by the shirt and throw him against the wall, and I knew I hated him, and I hated myself for hating him."

And what can we say about marriage? Matrimonial hopes may be the most optimistic ones we have. But we soon discover that the person we married is just that—a person, a human being with his or her own needs and expectations, some of which inevitably crash headlong into our own. The collision sometimes leaves no survivors, as evidenced by the percentage of marriages that end in divorce.

Mary Karr, in her memoir *The Liars' Club,* told about an uncle who, after a fight with his wife over how much money she spent on sugar, sawed their house in half, moved his half to the other side of the lot, and didn't speak to her for forty years. I wonder what might have happened had she ironed a hole in his shirt. Others may not literally split the house, but figuratively they do, as they allow conflicts and tensions and cold distances to create a separation almost as terminal as that decreed by a judge in family court.

The unhappiness we suffer with others can fill us with despair, guilt, anger, bitterness, hatred, regret, and more.

The Gift of Disillusionment

Are there any consolations to be found in this bleak situation? I believe there are, and they are two of the most important gifts we will ever receive.

The first is disillusionment. This doesn't sound appealing, I know, but think about what the word means.

Not long after failures of mine became publicly known, both my external and internal worlds collapsed. I tell about this in another book, *The Wisdom of Pelicans—A Search for Healing at the Water's Edge,* and there is no point in repeating it here, except to say I fell into depression, owing in part to self-recrimination and in part to the rejection I experienced from others. I had lost my job and was formally censured by the church, an organization I had spent twenty-five years serving and had believed was supposed to stand for forgiveness and mercy.

One evening I spoke with a wise friend, a retired hospital chaplain. I said, "Walt, I'm so disillusioned with the church."

He responded, "Don, have you ever thought about what it means to be disillusioned? What does the word literally mean?"

"Well . . . *dis*illusioned. I guess it means to lose one's illusions."

"Exactly," he said. "Why do we consider that a bad thing?"

We consider it a bad thing because it hurts. We have carefully constructed our illusions to protect us from reality. To explain what I mean, we must return to the real reason we fear all limitations—our terror of death.

Ernest Becker's oft-quoted *The Denial of Death* won the Pulitzer Prize in 1973, but it took me about twenty-five years to get around to reading it. Better late than never. It's a rare and, for me, indispensable book. It illuminates, with brilliant clarity, some of the darkest corners of human experience. Drawing chiefly on the philosophy of Søren Kierkegaard and the psychology of Otto Rank, Becker pulls together the most significant strands of post-Freudian psychoanalysis for an utterly persuasive argument that the terror of death is embedded deeply in our unconscious and influences us more profoundly than we realize.

Our life project consists in finding a way to live with this terror. The character we create for ourselves, even our neuroses and psychoses, is part of this endeavor. These things are like whistling in the dark, attempts to convince ourselves that we are not being stalked by an implacable foe.

One of the most important strategies we adopt is "to live on delegated powers," to transfer our hopes for defeating death to other persons. We all need to be "heroic," Becker says, to find a way to become immortal. On our own we cannot achieve this, so we project this burden onto others. We look to parents or lovers or political leaders or pastors or celebrities—there are many substitute heroes—to insure our safety and help us transcend death.

This transference is, according to Becker, a

taming of terror. Realistically, the universe contains over-whelming power. Beyond ourselves we sense chaos. We can't really do much about this unbelievable power, except for one thing: we can endow certain persons with it. The child takes natural awe and terror and focuses them on individual be-ings, which allows him to find the power and the horror all in one place instead of diffused throughout a chaotic universe. *Mirabile!* The transference object, being endowed with the transcendent powers of the universe, now has in himself the power to control, order, and combat them.

The terror of death may be tamed through this transference, but another problem emerges:

then he experiences "transference terror," the terror of losing the object, of displeasing it, of not being able to live without it. The terror of his own finitude and impotence still haunts him, but now in the precise form of the transference object. . . . The transference object becomes the focus of the problem of one's freedom because one is compulsively dependent on it; it sums up all other natural dependencies and emotions.

If we ponder Becker's words carefully, we will learn much about ourselves and our relationships with others. At the center of our being is a terror of *the* limitation, death. From infancy we're aware of our vulnerability in a dangerous universe. So to protect ourselves we construct patterns of behavior that we imagine (albeit unconsciously) will defend us against this terror. Because we know that we ourselves cannot defeat death and gain immortality, we shift our hopes to others. This transference, according to Freud, is a "universal phenomenon of the human mind." Unfortunately, it imprisons us in a constricting dependency.

Distorted Relationships

Our parents are the first we endow with power to protect us. They are "larger than life" or, to state it more accurately, larger than death. Therein lies the difficulty of separating ourselves from their influence. If I become like my all-powerful parents, I will be safe; if I leave them, I will be in danger.

For their part, our parents may well have consigned a good many aspirations to us. Biologically, their lives continue through us and our children. Psychologically, this creates a gravitational pull of almost irresistible force. Our achievements and experiences, as well as our genes, become a way for our parents to find some measure of immortality.

It's not hard to see why family relationships are often a mess, entangled in emotional complications despite genuine affection and self-sacrifice. What else can we expect when we do not relate to one another objectively, but only through the subjectivity of our own desperate needs?

The same could be said about our other relationships. Indeed, transference influences—perhaps I should say *distorts*—all our interpersonal transactions. We employ friends, coworkers, even casual acquaintances in pursuit of our "life project" of becoming a hero. To state it as starkly as possible, we do not relate to others as they are but as we need them to be for us.

Nowhere does this play out more dramatically, and sometimes more tragically, than in romance. Consider a woman who finds herself in an unhappy marriage. She appreciates her husband, even loves him. But they have grown apart and have little in common, and this has left a hole in her heart. It's more than painful: it's a reminder, albeit unconscious, of the hole—the nothingness—that she herself will one day be. She had invested many aspirations in her husband. Now she feels dangerously unprotected.

If she has the courage to face this limitation, to accept it as inevitable and to accept the gifts it has to offer, she may find herself rising above it. Instead, she becomes aware of a colleague at her office. He is good-looking, has a great sense of humor. They gravitate toward each other during breaks and find reasons to confer about projects, and the fact that he is also married doesn't seem relevant; after all, she is not planning to have an affair. He is just a good friend, someone who understands her. In his presence she feels new energy.

The energy she feels is *eros*, the inner movement toward beauty and goodness, toward greater wholeness, toward a larger embrace of life. It is also a flight from fear, especially death. So transference takes place. The man becomes her new purchase on salvation.

Eventually, she finds herself in the shower after an hour of sexual passion, an hour in which she seemed to find the other half of her being, and the hot water can't wash away the unexpected melancholy that descends. She is not sad, exactly; the ecstasy of union still lingers, and its memory is strong enough to hold off sorrow. But neither is she completely happy. She doesn't understand it. Is it because she must now go home and lie to her husband about a dull day at the office? Is it because guilt has pierced her heart? Is it because she knows she has turned into a cul-de-sac? Whatever else, it is surely this: she has an early intimation of a new bondage. She is now captive to her lover, and this dependency has stolen at least part of her freedom.

From Disillusionment to Detachment

With all this transference taking place, is it any wonder our relationships are troublesome? We *use* people for our purposes, conscripting family members and friends and colleagues into the army of our defenders. And they have most likely already conscripted us into their army! It's no wonder we face limitations in our relationships. Others cannot carry the load of our expectations; sooner or later they *must* disappoint us. As each relationship fails to provide what we want, we become more desperate and cry out with the kid and his saxophone, "Do you love me? Do you love me? Do you love me?" Hearing no convincing answer, the disillusionment grows.

This is really a gift. Disillusionment demands that we face the truth that other human beings cannot save us from our deepest fears, cannot make us secure in a dangerous world, cannot make us happy, cannot, in short, be gods for us. This hurts like hell. I mean this literally, for it feels as though we have been abandoned by the deities we have appointed for our salvation. We feel alone and godforsaken.

But here's the good news: it's the first step toward authentic love. Only as we are despoiled of illusory love do we find

40

the treasure of authentic love. The gift of disillusionment confers another gift, if we choose to receive it. That gift is detachment.

The writer Madeleine L'Engle puts it this way:

> To learn to love
> is to be stripped of all love
> until you are wholly without love
> because
> until you have gone
> naked and afraid
> into this cold dark place
> where all love is taken from you
> you will not know
> that you are wholly within love.

We cannot love others fully and authentically until we detach ourselves from others. This is another of the great paradoxes of life. So long as our "love" is really a tool of transference, an attempt to possess and control, we will never be able to give ourselves; so long as we turn others into substitute heroes to save us, we will be manipulators more than lovers.

If I transfer my prospects for happiness and salvation to my wife, I will lay upon her an impossible weight. She will inevitably become a failed god. If I insist on living with illusions, I will have to turn my back on her to find a more promising god, or keep hoisting her up on the pedestal of my dreams and flogging her into becoming a better god. But there is an alternative: I can turn my disillusionment into detachment, withdrawing from her for the sake of a deeper union, renouncing love for the sake of love. As she steps down from her pedestal and allows me to step off mine, we can relate to one another as unique individuals, giving of ourselves without the distortion of desperate manipulation and ulterior motives.

41

And you can be sure that if you have disillusionment, you've probably created plenty of the same in others. It's a sure bet that at least a few people are mighty unhappy with you. It's also a great relief. Well, not at first, of course, because it's a heady thing to be treated like a god. Is there anything—*anything*, in all the world—more intoxicating than having your children, to use one example, look up at you with eyes of absolute trust and confidence? For a while you almost believe you deserve the adoration; after all, for years you've protected and nurtured them. But let's lay the whole truth on the table: this is also a worrisome burden to haul around every moment of the day. It's not easy to be responsible for someone else's life and happiness. So it can be a great liberation—often coming after much misunderstanding and heartache and guilt—to be let off the throne.

Okay, so you weren't the parent your children wanted or thought they needed. Guess what? You're not God. And your children, too, are only human. Neither you nor they have the power to calm the deepest anxiety in a human heart or satisfy its most intense longing. What you do have, at this unavoidable limitation, is an opportunity to meet each other anew and learn to love more freely and fully and thus more joyfully.

What is true with children and parents is also true with spouses and lovers and friends and colleagues—with the other human beings around whose roots our own have intertwined. We cannot be God for them, any more than they can be God for us. The limitations inherent in this help us realize that though we need each other to live, this need is not *desperate,* not a grasping, clinging, manipulating need, but one that comes from being created for a love that can only be freely given and freely received.

Love flourishes only in freedom. Relationships based on the illusions born of insecurities inevitably will become coercive, and nothing destroys love faster than coercion.

How could it be otherwise? Love is a gift, one that cannot be given under compulsion or taken by force. Love cannot happen if others are treated as mere extensions of ourselves, as slaves of our needs and desires. Only through detachment—the separation of ourselves from others and others from ourselves—can we find the freedom that makes room for the mutual attentiveness and mutual honoring and mutual delight and mutual serving that are the foursquare foundation of authentic love.

4

Giving Up on the **New York Times** Crossword Puzzle

The Limitations of Knowledge

At the outset of this chapter, let us, as lawyers say, agree to a stipulation: most of us could exercise our brains more vigorously with no danger of straining them. Who of us would say we've maximized our cognitive potential, that we've come to the end of our capacity for learning and analyzing and thinking? It wouldn't hurt us to push our gray matter harder, even making it break a sweat now and then.

It's often been said that we use only about 10 percent of our brains. When I was younger, the thought of 90 percent of mine just lying there, lounging in my cranial hammock and knocking back beers, goaded me into one self-improvement resolution after another. It also provided serious comfort when, drinking my own beers, I worried that what a Sunday school teacher once told me might be true, that every swallow of alcohol kills off

44

brain cells that can never be regenerated. Even if I burned out 10 or 20 percent of them, I reasoned, I still had plenty to spare for all the learning I planned to do through my life.

But I recently read that it is a myth that we use only 10 percent of our brains. At this point in my life, the news came as a relief. After decades of programs that have produced—how shall I put it?—modest, barely discernable, advances in mental betterment, I'm tired of feeling like a slacker. Now that I know I've actually been firing most of my hundred billion neurons, each with its ten thousand different connections, I'm quite pleased with myself. Even amazed.

Until I try to remember where I put my keys. Then, it seems, some of my neurons aren't pulling their load. I don't know if I'm really forgetting more things or if I'm just *worried* about forgetting more things and thus more aware of it when I do. The front door of my brain has not shut; new information and ideas get in as easily as ever. But someone has left the back door open. Knowledge that once came in and made itself at home decamps faster than a barhopper in search of a more interesting place to hang out.

Two days ago, for example, I was trying to determine whether a new sofa would fit through a doorway in our house. I had two of the measurements I needed, and I knew—I could remember this much—that there was a formula for coming up with the third and that I had memorized it in tenth-grade geometry, no doubt right after Mrs. Haynes had said we would someday be glad we had learned what she was teaching us. Now, forty-three years later, that day had finally arrived, and I couldn't remember the formula to save my life. In such moments, I worry about Alzheimer's, of course, as those of us over fifty do every time we forget something. But I'm cheered by a distinction Hugh Downs made a couple of years ago, saying it's no big deal to forget where you put the keys, but you'd better be concerned if you forget what keys are for. I tell myself that not remembering some things is normal, because, after all, my brain has gotten pretty full over the years, and it's not at all surprising that a few items would escape without being noticed until they're needed.

But I plan to keep welcoming enough new knowledge to make up for what is escaping out the back door. I want to keep my brain as busy as a wild party. I don't see any reason to give up, even as I get older. Carl Sandburg wrote *Remembrance Rock* at seventy. Benjamin Franklin invented bifocals when he was seventy-eight. Sophocles wrote *Oedipus Rex* at seventy-five and *Oedipus at Colonus* at eighty-nine. Titian completed *The Battle of Lepanto* at ninety-five and began one of his best-known works, *The Descent of the Cross,* at ninety-seven. Grandma Moses was still painting at one hundred. Bertrand Russell was leading international peace drives at ninety-four. George Bernard Shaw wrote *Far-Fetched Fables* at ninety-three. Pablo Picasso was producing drawings and engravings at ninety. Albert Schweitzer headed a hospital in Africa at eighty-nine. Arthur Rubenstein gave one of his great recitals at Carnegie Hall at eighty-nine. There is no justification for an idle mind.

Walls of Ignorance

Nevertheless, every one of us faces limitations in knowledge. Without exception.

Albert Einstein eventually crashed into a wall of ignorance: his mind could push through to relativity theory, but it couldn't combine that with quantum theory into a unified field theory. He searched for this all-encompassing theory for the rest of his life, but it eluded him.

In more mundane ways, we all meet limitations in our abilities to reason and remember and reflect. As we age, this may become more apparent to us; "senior moments" or senility or Alzheimer's are dramatic, more extreme manifestations of something we experience throughout our lives. Our brains can absorb and process only so much, and whether we're sitting in geometry with Mrs. Haynes or in a wheelchair at a convalescent care facility, we have to accept the consequences.

Here's what I'm wondering: are there any good consequences? Are there consolations to cherish in this sad situation? What gifts do the limitations of knowledge grant?

Accepting Our Humanity

The most important blessing bestowed by our inevitable ignorance is the freedom to be human. That we need this may not be immediately evident. What other choice do we have?

Objectively considered, we can be nothing other than human. But in that deep place where desires push and pull and shape us, there lives a secret hunger to be something more than human. To state it bluntly, we want to be God, or at least *a* god, a know-it-all being who can control its own world.

Do you recall the story of creation in the first chapters of Genesis? Some believe it is literal history; others consider it an ancient myth, meaningless for the modern world; others—I'm included in this group—stake out a position between these extremes. However you view this piece of Judeo-Christian heritage, I invite you to ponder what it says about our human situation. Myths that have endured for centuries in our collective consciousness should never be taken lightly; they should be looked into, or perhaps looked through, like windows that make possible a clearer view into what it means to be a man or woman. The older I get, the more appreciation I have for myths of all kinds, especially those that have shaped the culture around me, and therefore shaped me, however much I may or may not be aware of it.

Despite what you might have been told, you don't have to set aside convictions about evolutionary biology to learn from

47

the Genesis story. It tells us that human beings are more than mere accidents in a universe of happenstance; they are part of something purposeful, something endowed with great meaning. A Creator has been at work and has fashioned us as rational, thoughtful creatures. The first man and woman were given responsibility to subdue the earth and to have dominion over the plants and animals. One way this dominion manifests itself is through naming. The story says that God, after forming the animals and birds, brought them before the man "to see what he would call them."

On the table next to me is a book entitled *Birds of San Diego County.* I like to keep it handy. Birds sometimes land on the trees outside my window. Yesterday, for example, a yellowish-orange one perched on a branch of a palm I stare at when I'm searching for the next sentence or just daydreaming, and I studied it as carefully as possible it until it flew away. Then I thumbed through my book to find its name. Why did I do this? I could have enjoyed its vibrant color and delighted in its movements without knowing that it was a Bullock's Oriole. But I wanted to learn this, and if, by some unlikely chance, I had been the first ever to see it, you can be sure I would have named it. Woven into the fabric of my species is a primitive need—a primeval *necessity*—to discover and learn and name and catalog. To be human is to be a scientist in search of knowledge.

Oddly enough, the same creation story tells us that God told the man and woman that they could eat the fruit of every tree in the garden, except one—the tree of the knowledge of good and evil. Violating this prohibition would incur a severe penalty ("in the day that you eat of it you shall die"). This command, not surprisingly, became the occasion for Adam's and Eve's first temptation and their oft-followed disobedience. The serpent was clever: "You will not die," he said, "for God knows that when you eat of it your eyes will be opened, and you will be like God, knowing good and evil."

You will be like God. The temptation that proved too enticing to deny was more than ripe fruit, however beautiful and delicious it might have been. The *really* desirable, impossible-to-resist part of the serpent's seduction was the promise of a promotion: *if you eat this fruit, you will gain knowledge that will make you more than human; you will be like God.* The *essential* temptation, this story says, the foundational snare to our humanity, is to want to be something other than we have been created to be, to want to rise up and take God's place.

Eve couldn't resist. She sampled the fruit and handed it to Adam, and he lost no time joining the repast. They could not accept a limitation to knowledge; they wanted to know more than was their right.

I have advanced degrees in theology, and I have reflected on this account of human origins for many years, but I don't claim to understand it. This much, though, seems clear: it shows a central dilemma of our human condition. We were made for learning, for the acquisition of knowledge. Yet, at the same time, we come to a boundary of knowledge that we pass over to our "death." To try to be God means the end of our humanity. To take the place of the Creator is to assume an impossible, unlivable burden.

The gift offered at the boundary is the freedom to be who we were meant to be—humans. We are not God, and thus we do not need to know everything, to explain all things, to answer every question, to solve all mysteries. Yes, to be human is to want to do these things, and part of our glory is to do them as fully as possible, so far as we are able, right up to the edge of the boundary. But the inevitable limitations to knowing remind us that we are not God, that some things are beyond our comprehension.

I don't want to imply that, in Einstein's case, for example, the unified field theory was his forbidden fruit, and that he would have discovered it to his peril. Some day a physicist will no doubt find it, expanding our intellectual horizons. But for now, this limitation, like all others, is a reminder that whatever heights we might ascend, we will never become God. Our limited knowledge tells us that we are humans, and though part of our glory is to keep searching and learning, part of it also is to accept that we are not God, that some things are beyond our ken, that we are surrounded by mysteries before which we can only be in awe.

Teachable Ignorance

This leads to an important affirmation: ignorance is a necessary part of being human. I'm not suggesting that, as descendents of Adam and Eve, our highest calling is to be intellectual couch potatoes, that we should not even begin Saturday's *New York Times* crossword puzzle, let alone worry about finishing it, that we should forthwith fulfill our destiny by dropping out of school, that we should quit expanding our understanding of the world around us. I do, however, want to stress that ignorance is a precondition for the most important discoveries.

Those who already know the truth may not be open enough to receive its new appearances; those who possess knowledge may not be empty enough to receive its new manifestations. There was a time when everyone "knew" the world was flat, but explorers like Christopher Columbus had the courage of doubt, and their agnosticism gave birth to astonishing discoveries. For fourteen centuries, scholars accepted as "knowledge" Ptolemy's theory that the earth was the motionless center of the universe, and then along came a doubting Nicolas Copernicus, who was open enough to imagine a different possibility, thus laying the foundation of modern astronomy. Significant learning is almost always preceded by someone saying, "Well, I don't know about that . . ."

Any teacher will tell you that the most difficult students to teach are those who already know it all. The ones most likely to learn have a teachable ignorance. This kind of ignorance is not the result of genetic stupidity or intellectual laziness or mental passivity, but is really a hungry emptiness and a willing receptivity.

Only in the darkness can you see the stars.

Reverent Receptivity

Some things—perhaps the most important—cannot be grasped, regardless of the reach of one's intellectual prowess. They can only be received. There is a knowledge that cannot be gained by thinking or reasoning or deducing or inducing or experimenting or theorizing; it comes *to* us, not *from* us, and it can only be acknowledged, with gratitude and surprise, when it appears in an open heart. We can prepare for this knowledge, paradoxical as it sounds, by encountering the limitations of knowledge. These limitations, by reminding us of our humanity and our relative ignorance, help create the awe and wonder necessary for encountering the deepest, most soul-shaping truths.

We cannot be fully human without reverence. To rise to our proper status but not vainly to aspire beyond it is to know our place, and what is that but the ground between the naming and the not-knowing? Our knowledge emerges between bold confidence and shy humility, in the place between the creation and the Creator. However much we might learn, we never graduate beyond the need for quiet reverence—that childlike wonder and considerate respect—for the things around us, from spider webs to Bach fugues, from the not-so-simple fact of our own being to the incomprehensibility of God. In this in-between place, if we wait with respectful openness, we may well hear voices speaking truths we could not have told ourselves, and behind them a Voice revealing Truth.

Standing in the shade of the tree of the knowledge of good and evil, we have a choice: we can pluck the fruit and do our best to storm the throne of heaven. Or we can kneel in humility, knowing we do not know, knowing we are nothing but creatures dependent on a Creator, knowing that whole universes of reality may exist beyond our powers of perception, knowing that, for the time being at least, we exist on the edge of a vast mystery.

Sometimes this is painful. In the presence of suffering we naturally ask *Why?* We want to pull back the curtain of mystery to look for answers. We think that if only we understood the reason for misfortune, we would find it easier to bear. We are mistaken. Rational explanations provide only short-term relief, at best. Recall the most painful season of your life. Perhaps your child died, or your spouse walked out on you, or in some other way a white-hot poker pierced your heart. If you had known the reason for what had happened, would that have taken away the hurt or the sorrow? I doubt it. The loss would have remained, a terrible vacuum at the center of your being mocking you with its persistence. But the question persists: *Why?* We would give almost anything for some mysteries to be even a little less mysterious.

This longing can spring up from the soul's depths in response to good things, too. When we are surprised by joy, as C. S. Lewis described a turning point in his life, or when we are embraced by an unseen arm of mercy, or when we are seized by an evanescent but real sense of an Other, or when we are overcome by something so wonderful we're afraid to mention it to anyone—when we are de-centered by ecstasy—we long for more of this strange, destabilizing beauty. We want to *know,* and now I am using the word in its biblical sense, in the way ancient writers used it as a synonym for sexual intercourse. The mystery fascinates us, draws us, and we want to penetrate it or be filled by it.

But it remains beyond our reach. Aggressive research and forceful reasoning may help us obtain knowledge of objects, but not knowledge of subjects, not the truth of personal beings. Relational knowledge can only be received as it is freely given.

However much a man might pursue a woman, for example, however much he believes he loves her and wants to learn everything about her, the door to her being will be bolted shut unless she unbolts it from the inside and willingly reveals the secrets of her life. Until that happens, all he can do is wait patiently and humbly, which is to say reverently, respecting the profound mystery of her being.

If this is true of our relationships with persons, how much more so with God. For here we have the Mystery behind all mysteries, the Wholly Other. How could the finite encompass the Infinite? How could our minds contain the One who contains all things? How could our hearts embrace the Heart of the Universe? Even if we listen to great sermons and lectures, read classics of philosophy and theology, employ flawless logic in deduction and keen observation in induction—even if we do everything in our power as rational beings—we will never get close to God, unless God comes close to us, unless God grants a self-revelation, unless God unlocks the door of our understanding. Christians say this has happened in Jesus Christ, and they *know* this because they have received it through faith. They have opened themselves, with reverence and humility, to truth that could only come *to* them from *outside* them.

The limitations of knowledge can open us to this kind of truth, if only we quiet ourselves long enough to listen.

5

On Not Being Elected President (or Member of the Condo Board)

The Limitations of Achievement

As a child you might have wanted to be an astronaut, a cowboy, and a doctor. Worthy occupations, all. But even if you had had the ability to land a space shuttle and herd cattle and remove a gall bladder, you wouldn't have had the time to do it all. Growing older means making choices. An increase in age inevitably means a decrease in certain possibilities.

But the drive to achieve remains long after we've had to compromise and adjust our dreams. Most of us want to accomplish things: we want to become vice president of sales, maybe, or join the school board, or organize a happy family, or buy a beautiful home, or build a financial portfolio. Our focus narrows, perhaps, but not necessarily the energy pushing us toward new accomplishments.

People vary in this matter, of course. When I was in seminary, I had to take a series of tests to determine my fitness for ministry. A few weeks later I met with a psychologist to discuss the results. On his lap were papers plotting my personality on a graph and quantifying it into numbers. "Don," he said, "how do you think you ranked in terms of mechanical interest?"

"Ah, pretty low, I suppose."

"Low? You're not even on the graph!"

This is why my wife considers it noteworthy when I change a lightbulb, and why, a couple of weeks ago, she wanted to hold a press conference when I installed new hardware on our front door. I wasn't sure what this particular flaw in my personality had to do with ministry, except to rule out a call to a small church where I would have to double as the custodian. It must be proof, I thought, that I was made for a large congregation where others would worry about leaking toilets.

The psychologist continued. "And how do you think you ranked among achievement-oriented personalities?"

Uh-oh. Just as I was imagining a prestigious congregation. "Fairly high?" I asked.

"Well, yes, I would say so. You're in the ninety-ninth percentile."

That probably explained why I wanted to be king of the world, at least king of *my* world. I mention this to show I have experience with achievement orientation, as the psychologists say, or to put it in a less hoity-toity and more honest way, ambition. Perhaps mine has been more intense than yours, but even if you didn't strive to be at the top of the class, you have probably wanted to accomplish worthy goals. Most people do, and there are reasons for this.

Striving for Self-Worth

We want to be all we can be. That sounds like a recent army recruiting advertisement, but the army knew what it was doing when it appealed to this common aspiration. The psychologist Abraham Maslow wrote of our need for "self-actualization."

Even if all other needs—physiological, safety, love, esteem—are satisfied,

> we may still often (if not always) expect that a new discontent and restlessness will soon develop, unless the individual is doing what *he*, individually, is fitted for. A musician must make music, an artist must paint, a poet must write, if he is to be ultimately at peace with himself. What a man *can* be, he *must* be. He must be true to his own nature. This need we may call self-actualization.

We want to do our part in subduing creation and naming animals; we want to participate in and contribute to the human endeavor in our own individual ways. The flame of this ambition can keep burning even into old age. When cellist Pablo Casals was ninety years old he still practiced four or five hours a day. When asked why, he answered, "Because I have the impression I am making progress." I would guess that he could not *not* practice; he could not *not* fulfill his potential.

There is also a more fundamental reason for our ambition: we long for some basis for self-esteem. We need to respect ourselves, to see value in our being, and we expend much personal energy in providing a reason to do so. To quote Maslow again, "All people in our society (with a few pathological exceptions) have a need or desire for a stable, firmly based, usually high evaluation of themselves, for self-respect, or self-esteem, and the esteem of others." By achieving worthwhile goals, we think, we will make ourselves worthwhile; by making a valuable contribution, we will make ourselves valuable.

It has taken many years to understand that much of my drive to achieve—the push to accumulate a load of degrees, to lead a large church, to be a seminary president, to lecture and preach around the country, to write books—has been done to establish my self-worth. There were other motives, certainly, and many were praiseworthy. But somewhere beneath my consciousness there was a hunger to be considered valuable by others and thus maybe also by myself.

As I write this chapter, the news media are focused on the accounting scandals of Enron, Tyco, Worldcom, Adelphia, and other corporations that have "cooked the books" and, apparently, misled investors. Part of the story is the greed of CEOs who paid themselves outrageously high salaries and cashed in stock options, leaving thousands of small investors with decimated pension funds. For most of us, it's hard to understand how anyone would think he or she was worth a hundred million dollars a year, or how anyone could actually live in a thirty-thousand-square-foot mansion, or why anyone would need four or five different residences, not to mention seventy-foot yachts. (Well, the yachts I can understand, though in my daydreams I never own anything much bigger than about thirty-five feet.) But I suspect it has less to do with accumulating money and possessions than with accumulating self-esteem points. Huge compensation packages and the toys they buy are mostly ways to keep score, to provide assurance of great achievement and thus of great personal worth. Not far beneath towering egos are little children needing reassurance that they are loved.

I believe this is the case with the now-notorious CEOs because I'm convinced it's the case for all of us. We strive, to one degree or another, to prove our worth to the rest of the world and most of all to ourselves. If we get elected to a coveted position, or if our salary rises to over a hundred thousand dollars a year, or if we get the promotion, or if we have a beautiful home with three well-behaved kids, or if we have an attractive spouse, or if our book hits the best-seller list—if we achieve goals we set for ourselves—*then* we will be "successful," which means we will have a secure place in this world.

Achieving these goals never provides the payoff we had expected, as anyone can tell you. The hole of desire is so much greater than any accomplishment can fill. So we keep throwing new things into it, hoping to fill the void and create a solid ground of self-esteem.

To understand what put us on this treadmill of striving and achievement and yet more striving for the sake of yet more achievement, we need to recall again the creation story. Do you remember why the first man and woman were tempted to eat of the fruit of the tree of the knowledge of good and evil? The serpent suggested that if they did, *they would be like God.* The primal temptation, as I said, is to ascend to God's place, to situate ourselves in the control room, to put ourselves in charge of our world. But we're like little kids who've gotten into our father's workshop and have been caught plugging in the power saw: no matter how much we pretend to know what we're doing, we're in big trouble. It's not easy running the world, and we don't need anyone to tell us we're not pulling it off very well—which beats our self-esteem thinner than a Swedish pancake. So what do we do? Try even harder! Strive for yet more accomplishments, pump up that self-worth, inflate that ego!

But to be God, or even *a* god, as I said in the last chapter, means the death of our humanity. The thing we fear most is this death. As Ernest Becker taught us, we try to transcend the final limitation by becoming heroes, by achieving immortality. We know we can't do it, as we've seen, so we transfer hopes to other people. But that doesn't mean we cease struggling for our own heroic deeds. We fight against death on many different fronts, all at the same time, and the battle for immortality is particularly fierce on the front of our achievements.

Roadblocks

We need achievements for self-esteem, and, more importantly, we need them to fight the terror of death. What would become of us without our accomplishments? Who dares get off the treadmill long enough to find out? But who manages to stay on without becoming exhausted?

Weariness can take us to the limitations of achievements, sometimes gradually, through a slow grinding down of stamina and will, through an accumulation of failed goals and unsatisfying successes, until driving ambition is driven out of our lives.

But often we come to these limitations because of circumstances, over which we have no control, that happen to us. The drive is still there, but a roadblock is put in our way. We're laid off work because of corporate "downsizing"; we must take a disability leave; we turn sixty-five and though we feel more like forty on the inside we're forced to retire; we make compromises that ultimately catch up with us, throwing us to the sidelines. It happens in different ways, sometimes so suddenly we find ourselves lying on the ground, stunned, unsure what hit us.

We might pick ourselves up, dust ourselves off, and attempt to carry on as though nothing had happened, but, limping along, we have to admit we were wounded worse than we realized. We are in pain; we have an inner disquiet that makes us feel like abandoned children who have no idea how to get home. This sense of lostness comes from a blow to our self-esteem; it happens because we're no longer sure who we are and where we belong. We had counted on achievements to give us value. Without them, what are we worth? We had even looked to our accomplishments to rescue us from death. Now what will become of us?

Discovering a New Self

There are consolations in such limitations. I know this, because I have experienced them. This man who was addicted to personal achievement, who was accumulating one success after another, who had the respect and admiration of many people, suddenly crashed into a wall of his own making. Compromises I had made with my own deepest convictions caught up with me, and I was forced to resign my position as president of a seminary.

Until then I never realized how inextricably intertwined my self-identity was with my professional life. I was grateful for the personal satisfaction I enjoyed from being a pastor and a seminary president, but I thought that I knew how to "sit loose in the saddle," that I had not let myself get confused about the difference between who I was and what I was doing. But head-knowledge is one thing; gut-knowledge is something else. Not until my job—and thus the arena for my achievements—was taken away from me did I realize how much I had allowed my self-worth to be built upon it. If I was not a pastor or seminary president, who was I?

It would take more space than remains in this chapter to describe my feelings of emptiness and confusion and uncertainty, even my doubts about God. But I can honestly say that, looking back on it, it was one of the best times of my life—best, not in the sense of happiness but of growth. If it weren't for the humiliation and suffering that attended it, I would wish the same experience for my family and friends. What I learned was something I should have known: *I am different from my achievements.* My value as a human being, I discovered, was not directly connected with accolades I won, or money I made, or respect I garnered; it was not something I could earn but only receive.

I became aware of this gradually, as the result of three things. First, life went on. The sun rose, the birds sang, the music of Mozart inspired. I could still make love and read novels and run along the beach and drink coffee in the morning and sip wine in the evening. I even caught myself, once in a while, in an inexplicably good mood, laughing for no reason at all. And it struck me with the force of an otherworldly revelation that all these things were gifts; they were great, undeserved, improbable blessings. They had been in my life before, but, being so busy working toward my goals, I didn't

60

always have the time, or perhaps take the time, to notice them. But with nothing much to do, I had to be content just to *be;* I began to enjoy the life that was handed me, regardless of my achievements.

Second, I was still loved. If I had been asked, before losing my position, if my family and friends would be faithful, I would have answered, *Absolutely!* Beneath the surface of my awareness, though, there must have been doubt, because when they proved it, when they remained loyal, some severely criticized for doing so, I was surprised. By their actions they said, *We love you for who you are, not for anything you have done or will do.* This obvious, unflagging commitment stunned me into deep gratitude. I felt undeserving of their love.

True, a few people I had mistakenly thought were friends disappeared. They were not the genuine thing, however; they related to me as pastor or president and had no use for me when I no longer played those roles. Those who stayed near, who continued to telephone, who volunteered stories of their own failures, who invited my wife and me for pizza at the last minute, who showed that nothing had changed in our relationship by continuing to tease me and mock my eccentricities—those who said in a variety of ways, *All right, you failed, so what? We still love you*—gave me the gift not only of themselves but, in a way, the gift of me. By their loyalty, I could actually begin to believe, in deep and unshakable ways, that I had worth and would always have it, no matter what I achieved.

Their loyalty became a symbol, a not-so-minor sacrament, of God's loyalty to me. This leads to the third, most important thing I realized. I had preached and written about God's love for twenty-five years; it had been at the core of my religious faith. But when circumstances stole my identity, God's love was confirmed in astonishing ways. It was no longer theoretical; it ambushed me with its concreteness, with its not-to-be doubted reality, with its palpable presence. To be sure, there were days when I doubted God's concern for me. I would grumble and moan and expound on how God could do a whole lot better running my life and maybe even the universe. But even then I sensed that God had shown up for my pity party. In retrospect, I can pray with the psalmist, "When my soul was embittered, when I was pricked in heart, I was stupid and ignorant; I was like a brute beast toward you. Nevertheless, I am continually with you; you hold my right hand."

When my achievements had fallen like sand through open fingers, and when I had no hope for grasping any in the future, I found myself upheld by grace. To use the language of my tradition, the eternal love I had believed was freely offered through Jesus Christ was indeed *freely* offered, with no strings attached, apart from anything I had done or not done. That meant I had value, I had worth, I had everything I needed for rebuilding my self-esteem on a far more trustworthy foundation.

I tell this story because I believe that when you encounter the limitations of your achievements, you, too, will likely be surprised by the same things. It will be hard, without doubt; the wound of self-doubt will be opened and your fear of death will be exposed. But then you will be in precisely the right circumstances to learn that life goes on, that your family and friends still love you, that God's love can be trusted. And the new self you are given will be better than the one you lost.

6

Yet Another Year without Winning the Nobel Peace Prize

The Limitations of Moral Goodness

Everyone wants to be good. No healthy person says, "I'm going to do my best to fail morally." The guy who recently cut you off on the freeway didn't resolve that morning to be a bonehead. The politician who took a bribe didn't say to herself, "You've been too honest lately, so get busy with some malfeasance." Even convicted criminals, I would guess, didn't align themselves consciously with evil. Deep in every heart resides a desire to do good, and more, to *be* good. The exceptions are rare enough to prove my point.

Then why is life such a mess? Why do newspapers and newscasts continually report shocking stories of violence and greed? Why can't you get through the day without running into, or being run over by, offensive people? Why do selfishness and meanness and jealousy and betrayal and ruthlessness surge around us and, truth to tell, deep within us? If we all want to be good, why are we so bad?

Once again, the creation story of Genesis describes our situation: something woven into the fabric of our humanity causes us to bite into the forbidden fruit. All other fruit in the garden may taste terrific, but of course the one we really want, the one that seems most beautiful and tantalizing, the one we think we can't live without, is the one we've been told we can't have. As it turns out, it's the one we can't live with, as we usually discover before the juice dries on our chin.

This wrongdoing has been described in different ways. The Judeo-Christian tradition refers to it as sin, the violation of God's authority; the culture speaks of it as immorality, the violation of accepted norms; the judicial system calls it crime, the violation of law. In every instance, it is falling short of expectations. And whatever heavenly or earthly beings we might hurt, we sense that maybe most of all we hurt ourselves. By breaking a command or norm or law, we also break an important part of ourselves. The fire of self-will blazes brightly, warming and dazzling us, but eventually it leaves us crawling through the blackened, charred remains of guilt and shame.

What was I thinking? How could I have done such a thing? I didn't mean to cause such hurt, really. I'm such a fool. We pummel ourselves with questions and accusations.

The blaze usually gets going with only a spark, nothing serious. No one sets out to burn the house down. No one says, "Today would be a great day to commit adultery and leave two families in a pile of rubble." But surely it wouldn't be all that reckless to flirt a little, or share a prolonged lunch, or maybe even indulge in a kiss or a hug—all carefully controlled. Just a match to light the darkness, to relieve the boredom. And since that seemed safe enough, how about a firecracker? Then maybe a Roman candle. Before you know it, the roof is ablaze.

All of us, sooner rather than later, have to acknowledge we're not who we wanted to be. Perhaps we haven't burned down any houses, but that doesn't mean we don't harbor a pyromaniac fully capable of igniting a conflagration. We may not actually jump into bed with the neighbor's spouse, but we've imagined it in detail and living color. We may not actually push knives into competitors' backs, but we've repeated harmful gossip about them. We may not actually beat up a spouse, but we've been carried away by an irrational anger that belittles and demeans; we may not actually rob a bank at gunpoint, but we've fudged on our taxes.

Sometimes we wave off an uneasy conscience with the rationalization that we aren't as bad as others, or that "everyone does it," or that the rest of our behavior, taken as a whole, is good enough to offset our minor offenses. Self-justifications like these, let's frankly admit, can help for quite a while, but eventually our choices catch up with us. Perhaps the weight of accumulated compromises becomes too heavy to bear; perhaps we are publicly shamed; perhaps we see the pain we've caused loved ones. Then the disquiet in the conscience turns into outright agitation, even violent conflict, and we're torn apart by guilt and shame.

Though none of the limitations discussed in this book is easy, this one is particularly painful. Few things hurt more than remorse over what we've done or failed to do. We had wanted to be better; we had wanted to live up to our own expectations, but we are in a pit of regret. How could something like this happen, anyway?

Into the Light

Psychoanalytic theory has enabled me to gain a fresh perspective on this matter, and, along with it, a deeper understanding of some of the conscious and unconscious dynamics of my own failures. Like every science, psychology creates models to explain reality. These should not be treated as absolute truth (though trailing behind every theory are dogmatic adherents), but as useful frameworks for making sense of the best evidence available. I believe Carl Jung's concepts of the *persona* and the *shadow* provide one such model.

We all must compromise our natural inclinations with the expectations of civilized society, he tells us. We must adopt a certain stance through which to relate to the world around us. Jung called this the *persona*, the name used for the masks worn by actors of antiquity. It enables us to define ourselves in different circumstances, as we assume the roles of parent, lover, student, friend, professional, and so on. It's a necessary accouterment of social life.

The *shadow*, on the other hand, is the side of our personality we display neither to the public nor to ourselves. In the words of psychotherapist June Singer,

> It is what is inferior in our personality, that part of us which we will not allow ourselves to express. The stronger and more rigid the persona, and the more we identify with it, the more we must deny the other important aspects of our personality. These aspects are repressed to the unconscious, and they contribute to the formation of a more or less autonomous splinter-personality, the shadow. The shadow finds its own means of expression, though, particularly through projections. What we cannot admit in ourselves we often find in others. If, when an individual speaks of another person whom he hates with a vehemence that seems nearly irrational, he can be brought to describe that person's characteristics which he most dislikes, you will frequently have a picture of his own repressed aspects, which are unrecognized by him though obvious to others. The shadow is a dominant of the personal unconscious and consists of all those uncivilized desires and emotions that are incompatible with social standards and with the persona; it is all that we are ashamed of.

We stuff into the dark corners of our unconscious the baser instincts, the embarrassing emotions, the shameful desires,

66

the dangerous vulnerabilities. We hide these things even from ourselves; they are, for the most part, the unacknowledged part of us, the shadow.

Here is an important rule: *the shadow will have its way with us.* One way or another, it expresses itself. You can erect barricades around it, through conscious disciplines and unconscious defense mechanisms, but the shadow will find a way to escape, disguising itself to infiltrate your behavior. You can banish it to the nether regions, but count on it, it will emerge where you least expect it and take a large bite out of your backside.

A man might harbor anger against his wife, for instance, and because this is a negative emotion, something that would cause guilt if he consciously thought about it, he buries it in the cellar of his personality and puts a padlock on the door. Now he can tell himself that he has nothing but positive feelings for his wife, that he is rarely even upset with her, let alone angry. But underground, the anger grows and throws around its weight. Maybe it slips out when the man is trying to put something else in the cellar, or maybe it finds a gopher hole through which it crawls to the surface. Somehow, it gets out. Maybe the man finds himself in an innocent little disagreement with his wife, when suddenly he explodes in wrath toward her, even feeling an urge to hit her. An hour later, he's deeply shaken. Where did this come from? What's wrong with him anyhow?

Or a girl is raised to believe that sex is dirty, even sinful. Her parents would never state this explicitly, the subject is too obscene to speak about, but their silence loudly implies this. So what does the girl do with her sexual urges? She buries them, stuffs them into the cellar, pretends they don't exist. But over time they intensify, eventually bursting into the daylight. Maybe it happens as a teenager, when, swept along by a raging river of hormones, she surrenders to promiscuous experimentation. Or maybe it happens in middle age; after years in a marriage with a sex life that can best be described as compliant and passive, she suddenly becomes the aggressor and throws herself headlong into an affair.

My point is, every human being, even the most outwardly moral, has a shadow, and this shadow *will* express itself. The attempt to understand this dark and hidden aspect of our personality is what some psychologists call "shadow work." It's never easy to expose it to the light of consciousness, but we can avoid much future grief and achieve greater wholeness if we make the effort. It happens through paying attention to the sudden quickening of our emotions, to our dreams, to our secret fantasies, to the things that most annoy us about other people, and, perhaps most of all, to the lapses in our ethical standards. When we stumble and fall headlong into failure, when we do something we never would have imagined ourselves doing, we have an opportunity to see what caused us to trip, and thus we have a wonderful opportunity, if we seize it, for personal growth.

Acknowledging the Whole Story

This leads to the consolations of moral imperfection. If we have the courage to acknowledge our immorality, if we "confess our sins," in the language of religious faith, we can move toward greater integrity. Integrity has to do with integration, bringing together the different, often contradictory, parts of our lives; it refers to a wholeness of personality.

First, we must acknowledge that we're a confusing mixture: loving and selfish, generous and stingy, encouraging and envious, hardworking and lazy, angelic and devilish; we are both light and shadow. We've done good things, and we've also, in the words of the well-known prayer of confession, "left undone those things which we ought to have done; and we have done those things which we ought not to have done." I used to consider this prayer too general to be of much value; confession,

I thought, should be specific. But now I see the wisdom of its vagueness. Who can see into the depths of the shadows? Who can name all the cantankerous, aggressive troublemakers in the cellar? By definition, they are in darkness, out of sight and out of mind, even though they are probably projecting themselves onto other people and causing other mischief. So, along with specific faults, we admit general failure, the things that, if we knew them, would cause us shame and sorrow.

This doesn't necessarily call for sackcloth and ashes; it doesn't mean ceaselessly beating breasts and drowning in tears and bewailing guilt. In fact, these responses may reveal an immature perfectionism that refuses to grow up and accept the brokenness inherent in human life. Confession may indeed lead to deep remorse, which can trigger intense emotional reactions. But in its healthy form this is more a wading through sorrow than a wallowing in it. For the most part, admission of wrongdoing should have a matter-of-fact quality to it. It says, "Yes, this is who I am. It's not all I am, for I have written some good parts to my story, too. Yet I can't deny my failure (and my propensity to further failure) any more than I can deny my blue eyes."

As someone who has had to do more than his share of this, I can testify that it's quite liberating. It's as though the two circles of one's personality—the good and the bad, the persona and the shadow—overlap, and the resulting almond shape becomes a place of integration, of wholeness, of holiness. The larger we make this almond-shaped space, the closer we come toward fulfilling our potential. So we admit failure, and we do "shadow-work," and we pray for courage to see ourselves as we really are. As we live in this tension, affirming our paradoxical nature, we find ourselves—somehow, surprisingly—lifted above it. Though we may not yet know it, we're actually being raised by the updraft of grace, about which I will have more to say in the next chapter.

69

When we crash into the limitations of morality, we're in good company. King David was an Old Testament character right up there in importance with Abraham and Moses. Because of the well-known stories about him, his name is often mentioned in conjunction with someone else: David and Saul, David and Goliath, David and Jonathan. And one that didn't make it into as many Sunday school lessons but which you have been waiting for, David and Bathsheba. Yes, the greatest monarch in Israel's history—the one described as "a man after God's own heart," the one so important in the grand scheme of things that one of his descendents, Jesus of Nazareth, was not ashamed to be called "the Son of David"—blew it.

You probably remember what happened, if not from the Bible, then from countless B-grade movies. One spring day David took a nap on the roof of his palace, a customary place to seek relief from the afternoon heat. Things got really hot when he noticed, in a neighboring courtyard, a woman bathing. The Bible says, with economy of expression, "The woman was very beautiful," which provides some encouragement to the imagination. David wasn't content to leave it with his imagination, though, and before long, she was sharing his rooftop couch.

Well, that was that, or so David thought. An afternoon fling, a couple hours of pleasure, and perhaps a brief spasm of guilt. These things happen, after all, and he had been under a lot of stress. Life goes on.

Then came word that Bathsheba was pregnant. This was inconvenient, to be sure, but not insurmountable. He didn't become king of Israel and unify the nation and defeat his enemies by being an unresourceful slacker. He knew how to get out of a jam. So he sent for Bathsheba's husband, Uriah, who had been at war, to hear how things were going on the battlefield.

"Thanks, my good man," David said, "and as long as you're in Jerusalem, you might as well go home for a couple days of R and R." But the only rest Uriah took was with the king's servants, and the recreation he refused. He wouldn't enjoy his wife's company while his comrades in arms were far from their own homes. David had counted on him being a red-blooded Israelite who, within minutes if not seconds, would be all over Bathsheba like a rug on the floor, but he had not counted on his loyalty.

David was *king*, and he would deal with this problem one way or another. So he sent a letter, via Uriah himself, to the commander of the army, ordering Uriah placed on the front line where he would be killed. And sure enough, an enemy's arrow soon took his life.

David was ready to put this unfortunate incident behind him. He would marry Bathsheba and raise their son and everything would be fine. Except his failure would not let go of him, or perhaps, better said, God would not let go of him until he had dealt with his failure. The prophet Nathan confronted him, holding up to his nose the full stench of his actions. David, to his credit, didn't deny it, didn't evade responsibility, didn't make excuses. He simply said, "I have sinned against the Lord."

Tradition says that David then penned the confession found in Psalm 51: "Have mercy on me, O God, according to your steadfast love; according to your abundant mercy blot out my transgressions . . . . For I know my transgressions, and my sin is ever before me." We can only speculate about the psychological dynamics within David. But I think it's safe to say, on the basis of the story itself, that this honest owning of moral failure enabled David to grow as a person. In addition to his talent as a military commander and political leader and sensitive poet and inspiring musician, he was also a broken human being, a man with a dark side, a man, moreover, who could (and did) commit adultery and murder. David the Great King was also David the Moral Failure, and it's not taking liberties with the text to suggest that an important part of why he was more beloved than any other king in Israel's history was precisely because he integrated these failures into his life and thus rose above the conceits of power to become a man of compassion.

One incident from later in his life illustrates this. When his own son, Absalom, tried to overthrow him and David had to flee Jerusalem, a man named Shimei hurled abuse at him, cursing and throwing stones. "Out! Out! Murderer! Scoundrel!" One of David's aides wanted to take off Shimei's head, which must have sounded like a good idea to everyone present. Except David. David said, "Let him alone, and let him curse; for the Lord has bidden him." What a remarkable response! David was walking through the darkest valley of his life: his own son wanted to kill him, he was fleeing the city he had founded, he was losing everything he had worked to build. In this abject humiliation he revealed his true greatness; when his authority was most eroded he showed himself most kingly. He seemed to be on a different plane, higher than the conflict swirling around him. With little external power, he demonstrated internal power. And when eventually he returned to Jerusalem to reclaim his throne, Shimei came groveling for mercy, and, as you might expect, an aide once again wanted to send Shimei's head rolling, but David removed nothing more than Shimei's fear, offering compassion and forgiveness.

Perhaps David could be tolerant because many years before he had come to the same conclusion about himself: he *was* a murderer and a scoundrel. What Shimei meant as abuse, and what David's aides saw as disrespect, David could receive as simple truth—a truth, moreover, he had already incorporated into his life and thus had no need to hide or fear.

We shouldn't leave the story of David without remembering something significant: from a relationship begun in immorality, from the union between David and Bathsheba, came the great King Solomon, and after him came king after king, until one day, centuries later, came a different sort of king, one born in a stable, one who died on a cross, one who commands the loyalty of countless followers, one who is called the Savior of the world, Jesus the Christ. From the darkness of David's failure came forth the Light of the World.

Easier on Others

David's reaction to Shimei underscores another important consolation of owning our moral imperfection: tolerance. Those who have faced the complexity of their own lives, who have stumbled and fallen and been humiliated by their failures, have a more gracious spirit toward other people. They understand that things are rarely black and white, but more often varying shades of gray.

When I was a pastor, I soon learned that younger members of the congregation—especially those with small children—were more rigid than older ones. They seemed to crave clear, unmistakable boundary lines, and they often wanted me to be firmer in my preaching. They wouldn't have considered themselves judgmental, only concerned that Truth be upheld and Right Behavior required. They had lived just long enough to sense that living may be more complicated than they had thought, and this made them afraid, I think, for themselves and their children. They wanted the protection of law; they wanted a world of "good guys" and "bad guys"—with the "bad guys" nailed to wall and posing no threat.

But older members had been through a few more things. As Mark Twain said, "Anyone who has had a bull by the tail knows five or six things more than someone who hasn't." And those who have held on for a while have had to deal with—how shall I put this delicately?—more than a little of what emerges from that end of the bull. They are not terribly surprised or offended by life's manure, perhaps because they have dropped enough of their own along the way.

A few nights ago, I watched a televised interview with Art Linkletter. He had just turned ninety, and the host, Larry King, asked if there were any benefits to getting older. Linkletter responded immediately, "Yes, you become more tolerant."

One of the gifts of coming to the limitations of moral goodness is a gracious spirit. Knowing we need others to understand us, we can be more understanding; knowing we must count on the compassion of those who have endured our failures, we can be more compassionate; knowing we stand in need of much forgiveness, we can be more forgiving.

7

Don't Expect a Halo
on My Portrait
The Limitations of Spirituality

As a boy, I attended church not only on Sundays (morning and evening), but also on Wednesday evenings. If your father was the pastor, you were present whenever the lights were on, even during the week when you should have been busy with homework. Going on Sunday evenings was bad enough, because it meant missing the best TV programs of the week, though if I hustled I could get home in time for *Bonanza*. But having to show up for midweek prayer meeting was more than should have been required of someone who had put in a long day in school.

I was always there, however, along with about thirty of the most devout in the congregation. When the prayer service began, we got on our knees. We did not use padded kneelers attached to the back of the pew in front of us; that would have been too formal, something done by Catholics, Episcopalians, and Lutherans, and thus only marginally Christian. We had a hardier piety that got down on the floor, turned our butts around, and bowed our heads over folding chairs.

There were different styles for this. Most rested their elbows on the seat, either folding their hands or using them to cradle their faces. But a few of us folded our arms on the seat and dropped our heads all the way down. This posture had two distinct advantages: it implied a devout fervency, almost an anguish of spirit, and it was more comfortable.

Comfort was not what I needed at nine o'clock in the evening. I needed my feet in ice water. With head down and eyes closed, it was hard to stay awake. This created a problem when it came time to get up. Everyone else knew when to do this; they had an uncanny sense for rising in unison. This was as mysterious to me as salmon returning to the river of their birth, and I never figured it out. So I had to stay alert for the sounds of blowing noses and shuffling, which wasn't easy when asleep. As everyone slid up into their chairs again, and then stood to sing a closing hymn, I'd still be kneeling, obviously a very spiritual boy, obviously a true prayer warrior, obviously a Young Man of God. That I was actually dreaming, often about girls, created within me a kind of spiritual inferiority complex. How could I fall asleep when everyone else was praying? I felt like a phony.

That was just the beginning. Eventually I became a pastor, and others considered me a religious man. To myself, though, I was always that boy who couldn't stay awake. I was being used by God, it seemed; people profited from my preaching and counseling and other pastoral ministrations. But if a portrait had been painted to reflect my self-perception, it would have shown a halo that had fallen around my neck and an embarrassed grin on my face, as though I had just been caught in flagrant hypocrisy. I didn't think my prayers had any more effect than anyone else's, and most of the time I was sure I needed more help than my congregation.

I was a pastor long enough to learn that my feelings were not uncommon. My parishioners often confessed that they felt like spiritual failures; they seemed to be struggling to jump toward God but couldn't get off the ground because of an insurmountable gravitational drag. They were worn out by a never-ending cycle of optimistic promises and tailspin crashes, and they felt unworthy. The ones who didn't feel unworthy, who thought they had their spiritual ducks in a row, were not in as good a shape as they thought; believe me, you wouldn't have wanted to be around them.

The desire to get off the ground, to touch the transcendent, is not limited to members of churches or synagogues or mosques. According to opinion polls, more than 90 percent of Americans believe in God or a God-equivalent (e.g., a "higher power"); around 80 percent say that prayer is an important part of their lives; about 45 percent regularly attend worship services. These days, it's nearly impossible to hear an interview with a rock star or politician or you-name-it without hearing something like this: "I'm not religious but I'm very spiritual." It's not clear to me what this means, but I gather it's a disavowal of traditional institutions and an affirmation of a private spiritual life. Perhaps you, too, would say the same thing. But whether you're waving arms with Pentecostals or burning incense with Catholics or sitting properly with Presbyterians, whether you're meditating to find enlightenment or praying toward Mecca, whether you're communing with nature or chanting in the light of a full moon—whatever form your religious practice takes—you probably want to be on speaking terms with the divine, to feel that between you and God things are okay, to sense that you have in some way touched the mysterious forces of life or been touched by them. I would guess that you want to grow spiritually, that there is a part of you doing its best to get off the ground.

I would also guess that you're not finding it easy to fly. You could probably say with Carl Sandburg, "There is an eagle in me that wants to soar, and there is a hippopotamus in me that wants to wallow in the mud." You are undoubtedly acquainted with the limitations of spirituality.

A Surprising Declaration

St. Augustine, in *The City of God*, explained both the cause and the consolation of these limitations: "Adam himself lies now scattered on the whole surface of the earth. Formerly concentrated in one place, he has fallen; having been broken to pieces, as it were, he has filled the universe with his debris. However, God's mercy has gathered together from everywhere his fragments and by fusing them in the fire of his charity, he has reconstituted their broken unity." Spiritual limitations, he tells us, inhere in the human condition. Adam's disobedience (eating the forbidden fruit) and his arrogance (trying to be like God) have spread to all his descendents. His rising up caused his falling down, and we're all part of the wreckage. We can't rise up to touch transcendence because we're too broken, too shattered; our reach is simply not long enough to take hold of God.

But here is the good news: God's mercy has done what human effort could not do. God has gathered—and is gathering—the broken fragments into a new unity. The limitations of spirituality leave us no choice but to trust this work of God. They force us to rely on grace.

In his famous Sermon on the Mount, Jesus said something that, if it weren't for our familiarity with it, would strike us as exceedingly odd, maybe even wrongheaded: "Blessed are the poor in spirit, for theirs is the kingdom of heaven." Wouldn't we expect him to say, "Blessed are the *rich* in spirit . . ."? Wouldn't we expect him, of all people, to declare happy those who have cultivated a powerful spirituality, who have both the gifts to help others and the inner resources to draw upon in

78

their own time of need? But he proclaims happy the *dis*pirited ones; he congratulates those who in the world of the spirit feel like Tijuana garbage pickers.

The Greek word for "poor" in this text comes from the verb meaning "to cower" or "to cringe." It refers to the abject poor, not simply to those who wish they had more. It refers to those who long for *something*, to those who lack the wherewithal to cope, to those who have reached bottom, to those who have tried—again and again!—to be closer to God but find themselves a long way from home.

The poor in spirit don't consider themselves saints; they feel ineffective in prayer, and, for that matter, totally unworthy of the Almighty's attention. When others testify to spiritual victories, to signs and wonders and ecstasies, the poor in spirit want to crawl under the pew.

Why, then, would Jesus call people like this "blessed"?

Theirs is the kingdom of heaven! The arrangement of the words in the Greek sentence emphasizes that the kingdom—the rule of God in all its life-giving and healing power—exists precisely for the spiritually poor. This is because the rule of God is the rule of grace.

Blessed are those who come to the limitations of spirituality—and the sooner the better! For they have no other option but to rely on God's grace.

Trusting Grace

Of course, it makes all the difference whether there really is grace enough to trust. You might need it and hope for it, but if it doesn't exist you're in trouble. If the rule is that you have to earn your own way, that you have to work to prove yourself worthy, that you have to pull yourself up by your own bootstraps, well, to put in bluntly, you're in deep trouble. You have no alternative but to keep sweating and straining your way toward God.

On the other hand, if grace is the foundation of all reality, the bedrock on which the universe exists, then you're home free before you decide to leave the far country. You can take a deep breath, put your feet on the coffee table, and laugh with more freedom and good cheer than if you had won the lottery.

Now, in this regard, I can only speak from my own faith tradition. Christianity is based on the teaching of Jesus, the one who blessed the *poor* in spirit. His birth, life, death, and resurrection proclaim one central, astonishing truth: *God is love*.

If Jesus really is the self-revelation of God, as Christians believe, then God's way of being is grace; God's essential character is mercy; God's eternal movement is toward us and for us. Grace means we're already embraced before we can think about reaching toward God. Grace means we're forgiven before we're aware of our failures, let alone sorry and repentant. Grace means God is the Hound of Heaven, to use Francis Thompson's image, relentlessly chasing us down the days and nights of our existence. Grace means we have nothing to fear, not even the deepest, most troubling fear of all, death. Grace means that everything is turned upside down, or maybe turned right side up for the first time.

Brennan Manning refers to a scene from the play *Gideon*, written by Paddy Chayefsky:

> Gideon is out in the desert in his tent a thousand miles from nowhere, feeling deserted and rejected by God. One night, God breaks into his tent and Gideon is seduced, ravished, overcome, burnt by the wild fire of God's love. He is up all night, pacing back and forth in his tent. Finally dawn comes, and Gideon in his Brooklyn Jewish accent cries out, "God, Oh God, all night long I've thought of nuttin' but You, nuttin' but You. I'm caught up in the raptures of love. God I want to take You into my tent, wrap You up, and keep You all to myself. God, hey, God tell me that You love me."

God answers: "I love you Gideon."

"Yeah, tell me again, God."

"I love you, Gideon."

Gideon scratches his head. "I don't understand. Why? Why do You love me?"

And God scratches *His* head and answers, "I really don't know. Sometimes, my Gideon, passion is unreasonable."

Like Gideon, I don't understand why God loves me—or anyone else, for that matter. But does a minnow have to understand the ocean to swim in it? Does a goose have to understand his instinctive urges to fly south in winter before taking flight? Does a hawk understand the physics of hot air rising to soar atop the currents? Do I really need to understand the height and breadth and depth of God's love to throw myself upon it?

Authentic spirituality, it seems to me, does not depend on understanding everything about ourselves and God and then using that knowledge to hoist ourselves to a higher level of experience and achievement. Neither does it depend on cajoling God into doing something we think needs to be done. Authentic spirituality confidently assumes that God is up to something good, going ahead of us, calling us, embracing us, and it seeks simply to participate and delight in this.

If Gerard Manley Hopkins was not correct in saying, "We are wound/With mercy round and round," then I'm in big trouble. But if so, it's the best news I've heard. Most days I get out of bed believing it, and this enables me to accept, with equanimity and even joy, the limitations of my spirituality.

We all must decide: we can rely on our own spiritual striving, which turns every limitation into a hurdle to be overcome, if not a terrifying reminder of separation from God, or we can trust the grace of God, which turns every limitation into an occasion for further wonder and gratitude.

8

When the Roses Wilt
The Limitations of Romance

A recent issue of *Esquire* magazine had a one-paragraph article that caught my eye. Above it was a photograph of a scene from *I Love Lucy,* with Lucy and Desi seated on their respective twin beds. The first sentence began, "I hate sleeping with my wife," a sentiment one doesn't expect in the pages of that periodical. So I read on:

> I love her, mind you. And I think we've got a solid marriage. It's just that during those eight hours when our eyes are shut and we're drooling on our pillows, I want nothing to do with her. I came to this truth gradually. First I made her give up spooning; we're adults here. Then I went horizontal, across the bottom of the bed. Now I'm spending nights in the living room on the pull-out couch. In a couple months, I may just move to a separate land mass. I can't proselytize enough about this. I now snore with impunity. I toss and turn without waking her. I stay up late and read. I'm never accused (justly,

actually) of being an illegal occupying force in her mattress territory. Not even those 14-foot-wide, dictator-sized beds give you that peace of mind. I've come to realize that those privacy-loving Victorians had some good ideas, not counting that imperialism thing. And so did my parents, who preferred the more moderate but still workable pushed-together-twin-beds-option. When I was growing up, I always thought they were odd. Now I understand my mother's wisdom: "You don't use the same toothbrush. Why would you want to use the same bed?"

There was a time, I imagine, when the author would have expressed very different feelings. With the fires of romance blazing hot, he would likely have predicted that nothing would separate them in the night—no drooling or snoring or flailing, not even an invading army. They were united in body, mind, and spirit—so much so that their unity would withstand any threat. Eventually, though, the flames burned out. Practical realities, undistorted by runaway emotions, made it reasonable to sleep not simply in separate beds but separate rooms. They had reached the limitations of romance.

These limitations are universally acknowledged—and just as universally ignored, at least in the ecstatic seizures of passion. Well, of course. Few things are more pleasurable. Bertrand Russell, in his autobiography, speaks of his quest for romantic love:

I have sought love, first, because it brings ecstasy—ecstasy so great that I would often have sacrificed all the rest of life for a few hours of this joy. I have sought it, next, because it relieves the loneliness—that terrible loneliness in which one shivering consciousness looks over the rim of the world into the cold unfathomable lifeless abyss. I have sought it, finally, because in the union of love I have seen, in a mystic miniature, the prefiguring vision of the heaven that saints and poets have imagined.

83

Indeed, Russell's ecstasy does prefigure heaven, which is part of what gives romance so powerful a hold on us. But before looking forward to its consummation, we would do well to look backward to its inception, all the way back to the earliest days of our existence.

At that time, psychologists tell us, we did not distinguish between ourselves and the universe. The baby "cannot distinguish itself from the crib, the room and its parents. The animate and the inanimate are the same. There is no distinction yet between I and thou. . . . There are no boundaries, no separations. There is no identity."

Eventually, however, the child begins to experience itself as a separate entity. "When it is hungry, mother doesn't always appear to feed it. When it is playful, mother doesn't always want to play. The child then has the experience of its wishes not being its mother's command." This growing sense of differentiation enables the development of ego boundaries, the sense of an independent self.

But ego boundaries, however necessary for psychological growth, create problems. At a conscious level they make us lonely, imprisoning us within our individuality, making us want to connect with others. And at a deeper, unconscious level, they exacerbate our feelings of vulnerability in a dangerous world. As Ernest Becker taught us (recall chapter three), this sets in motion a lifelong process of transference, whereby we delegate power to parents and others in the attempt to find protection from the terror of death.

Falling in love allows a temporary escape from this. As Scott Peck put it,

> The essence of the phenomenon of falling in love is a sudden collapse of a section of the person's ego boundaries, permitting one to merge his or her identity with that of another person. The sudden release of oneself from oneself, the explosive pouring out of oneself in the beloved, and the dramatic surcease

of loneliness accompanying this collapse of ego boundaries is experienced by most of us as ecstatic. We and our beloved are one! Loneliness is no more!

In one respect, then, the pleasure of romance is regressive, enabling once again the oneness we felt in our mother's arms. But it is also a fulfillment, though only partial and temporary, of our longing for deliverance from fear, our hope for salvation from death, our hunger for transcendence. And thus Russell's description is more than poetic—it's literally true. The collapse of ego boundaries unifies us with the universe, and thus we have again that security we felt briefly as infants and have longed for ever since, that wholeness toward which our religious aspirations propel us.

When Candlelight Sputters

Alas, ego boundaries must snap back into place. We are no longer babies at the breast; we are not yet in heaven. We are individuals who must make our own way through this world, individuals who have no choice but to collide with other individuals doing the same thing. Even the one with whom we have fallen in love, who has made possible rapturous ecstasy (the original Greek word—*ekstasis*—meant "to stand outside oneself"), will one day become an individual with ego boundaries that impinge upon us, an individual who leaves spittle on the pillow, keeps us awake with a fine rendition of rocks rolling across a tin roof, and even knocks us in the nose with dream-induced punches. So when the lovemaking is finished and it's time to go to sleep . . . well, perhaps Lucy and Desi were on to something.

The discomfort of another's body competing for space next to yours is only the beginning. More difficult is the personality that comes with the body. The beloved other is just that: *other*—a person with ideas about how to squeeze the toothpaste tube and spend money and discipline the children, and when to invite the relatives and have sex and clean the house. Negotiating these differences can be more challenging than self-help books lead you to believe.

Philip Simmons honestly wrote of the contradictions in his own marriage:

> Funny how I can miss my wife terribly all day until the moment I walk in the house. We have a wonderful marriage, but some days it seems that the whole point of long-term relationships is to give people time to learn to torment one another efficiently. We become athletes of insult, proud of our ability not just to inflict pain but to do so with minimum effort. We know a relationship is fully developed when with a single lifted eyebrow we can ruin someone's entire day.

Simmons makes his point with exaggeration, but not much. There comes a time in every relationship when the candlelight sputters and the roses wilt. True, romance sometimes rises from the dark grave of the routine; the best relationships work at this, intentionally lighting new candles and cutting fresh roses. But new romance, too, will eventually come to a standstill against its limitations. The boundaries of the ego must—*must*—snap back into place, leaving us once again imprisoned in loneliness and longing for someone to save us from our deepest terror.

From Romance to Love

What consolation might be found in these dying embers?

Nothing less than this: *the limitations of romance encourage a deeper, more authentic love.* When you're no longer lifted and carried along by passionate emotions, you will be dropped on your face. Then you have a choice: either you can stay there, accepting the death of the relationship, or you can get up and walk on your own. If you choose the latter, you will have to do something, and that *doing*, that walking again with pain and determination, requires commitment. And this commitment is the necessary precondition for the highest and most rewarding form of human love.

How can we love fully without knowing our beloved?

How can we know our beloved without spending time with him or her?

How can we invest time in our beloved without enduring much—much happiness and sorrow, much laughter and tears, much hope and despair, much passion and disgust, much confidence and doubt, much faith and despair?

Every person is complex, layered with mysteries that are revealed slowly and through different circumstances. If we wish to know another intimately, we must wait and be attentive and endure, and this means outlasting the romance that initially drew us together.

This is why marriage is usually necessary for such love to grow. The binding promises before God and family and friends, sanctioned by law, create a network of obligation, a social contract that gives a relationship a fighting chance to develop into love. Romance may bring us together, seducing us into pledging ourselves to one another, but thereafter this covenant supports the love, almost like a fence that prevents us from fleeing at the first sign of trouble.

As I write this chapter, forest fires are blazing in western America. Hundreds of thousands of acres are being consumed by flames, and from my house I see a sky darkened by clouds of smoke from the "Pines fire" east of Julian, California. Some say we're having so many devastating fires because we've been too quick to extinguish appropriate fires, those that thin forests and clean them of underbrush. Redwoods, for example, need fire: fire scars and damages some trees, to be sure, but it also protects; it removes competition from the environment, leaving trees with the nutrients they need to mend themselves and flourish. For many years the forest service vigilantly put out fires among these giants, but an observant ranger noticed that where there were no fires, there were no new trees. Research revealed that cones open most fully in the heat of a blaze, dropping seeds on ash-covered soil cleaned of leaves and branches and fallen trees.

Something like this happens in a committed relationship. Trouble can burn through two lives, with much pain and scarring, seeming to bring nothing but destruction. But the heat can allow seeds of mature love to fall into richer soil and grow into something beautiful, something that will, in time, itself be life-bearing.

As a pastor I had opportunities to observe people in many situations, and I often witnessed couples who had been together long years as they walked or did their best to crawl through the valley of the shadow of death. The husband might be lying in a coma with a respirator keeping him alive. The wife would be next to him, caressing his forehead, whispering into his ear, telling him how much she loved him. And in the long moments of silence, I would imagine their wedding, the promises made with too much optimism and the unfolding of it all: the early disagreements that became arguments that became outright fights; the seasons of mind-numbing thus-and-so-ness when not much of anything happened, least of all romance; the betrayals and tearful requests for forgiveness; the woman, maybe, standing with her bags packed, ready to walk out the door but finally unable to go anywhere but back to the life she had chosen for herself; the sleepless nights in which they each wondered whether it was worth the struggle. I would imagine all this and more, and I knew that if they were like most couples, I was not far from the truth of their lives. But there they were, with a love that could only have been possible because of all that had shaped and challenged and wounded it, a love deep and spacious, a love that had so hallowed the hospital room I felt as though I should take the shoes off my feet and bow my head in reverence.

A love like this can happen only, I believe, when romance dies. Losing ego boundaries and becoming one with another may be wonderful, to be sure, an experience to cherish. But there is something better than union with another person: it is *communion* with another person.

Union with another is thrilling because it satisfies my needs. It releases me from the prison of my individuality, it delivers me from my loneliness, it enables me to project my longings for salvation from my unconscious terror of death; it makes possible regression back into my mother's arms and even intimates a death-defying transcendence. But believe it or not, there is a greater love. This love reveals itself in self-giving, in extending oneself *for the sake of the beloved.* The Greeks called this *agape,* the word used by the writers of the New Testament to describe the sacrificial love of God they had seen revealed in Jesus Christ. It is other-directed and aims to help the beloved heal and grow into the fullness of life.

To love in this way asks me to recognize the "otherness" of the beloved, that she is not an extension of my desires but a separate individual with needs and desires and a God-blessed uniqueness. When I grant her this honor and commit myself to helping her grow, I'm not *falling in love* but *building in love,* and out of this emerges a relationship more profound and joyous than the fleeting pleasures of romance.

Actually—this is something of a paradox—when I'm willing to let go of romance, accept its limitations and roll up my sleeves to do the heavy lifting of constructing a lasting relationship, romance sneaks back into my life with even more intensity and joy. The reason is obvious: now the passion flows from a knowledge of and respect for the other, now it's less a loss of self in the beloved than a giving of self to the beloved, now it's less an ecstatic absorption than a fulfilling fellowship.

Contrary to Russell's ecstatic vision, Christians do not view heaven as a perpetual state of mystical union. Some religions do embrace the ideal of absorption in the divine All. But those who look forward to the consummation of love revealed in Jesus Christ hope for something else: an eternal self-giving and other-receiving, a dance of individuals moving with a rhythm of bestowing and getting, committing and accepting, granting and gaining. In all the giving there will be no losing, and in all the receiving there will be no possessing. The Christian vision is not of union but of *communion*—a fellowship of personalities who do not disappear but finally find themselves in the being of Love Eternal.

When we come to the limitations of romance, we have an opportunity, if we have the courage and endurance, to grow into a love that will enable us to experience, even now, a small piece of this heaven.

9

Two Cheers for
the Little Blue Pill

The Limitations of Sex

I was tempted to leave this chapter blank. The pleasure of sex makes it hard to imagine how there could be consolations in its limitations.

Sex was one of the Creator's best ideas. Few things offer more delight: the bodily pleasure of tension and release; the adventure of exploring and knowing another human being; the real, if temporary, liberation from fragmented individualism into intimate communion. In a life often marked by frequent boredom, dreary routines, and hard labor, sex is a blessed interruption—perhaps I should say, a volcanic eruption—of ecstatic joy.

But it, too, has limitations. The most obvious is its dependence on bodies, and these bodies, as we've already acknowledged, must contend with the wear and tear of age.

A friend recently asked a small group of us, "Do you know the best birth control after the age of forty?"

Different answers came to mind but the smile on his face asked us to play along with him. "No, tell us."

"Getting naked."

We laughed, of course. We laughed because we were all over forty and had our share of wrinkles and flab and moles and plumbing problems; we laughed to distract ourselves from the anxiety that had been evoked; we laughed because that's often the best strategy for disarming a threatening truth.

But with our spouses standing next to us, we did not laugh too hard.

It's common knowledge that sexual vigor diminishes with age. Or at least, it *has been* common knowledge. Now we're questioning this. Research focused on older persons has provided a more accurate picture, one that reveals men and women in their sixties and seventies, even eighties, enjoying an active sex life. Yesterday, in preparation for writing this chapter, I thumbed through sections of *The Hite Report on Male Sexuality,* and I was enormously cheered to discover what many retired people do with their spare time! The consensus among Hite's interviewees seems to be that though sexual activity changes over time, its desire and pleasure remain. Reading about this reminded me of something my white-haired dad likes to say: snow on the roof doesn't mean there can't be fire in the furnace.

Still, most couples report *some* flagging of interest and performance over time. And, regardless of age, even the most ready-to-get-it-on couples have to admit inevitable limitations. They may shake loose the bedsprings three or four times a day, but there comes a time when even champions of libido need a break. The body can take only so much pleasure. Besides, the bills need to be paid and the garbage taken out.

And many are simply not able to have sex, no matter how much they want it. Perhaps they're single, with no romance in their lives; perhaps their spouses are ill or uninterested; perhaps they can't transcend debilitating emotional hurdles; perhaps they're too wounded from past experiences; perhaps they have no energy left after raising children and making a living. There are many reasons why people undergo involuntary celibacy. In fact, it's fair to assume that all of us, at one time or another, endure this.

The limitations of sex are so obvious, I hardly need to belabor the point.

A Welcome Respite

So what possible consolations could be found in the diminution of something so wonderful?

For one thing, these limitations provide time to think about other things. Meager compensation, you might say. But consider this: the average male thinks about sex six times an hour. On a slow day. Now, if you deduct eight hours a night for sleep, much of which is spent dreaming about sex, and multiply the remaining sixteen hours a day by a lifetime of seventy years, you end up with 2,446,080 thoughts about sex. This is the average, as I said. Which is why some of you are now thinking, *Only six times an hour? Some of the brothers aren't pulling their load!*

I wouldn't presume to speculate how often women think about sex, but if the statistics are anywhere near the other half of the species, it's a wonder the human race has had the mental wherewithal to build bridges, write novels, and perform open heart surgery. We should probably thank the limitations of sex for these things; they provide a valuable service, releasing us, at least briefly, to be more attentive to other things—things good and beautiful and productive but without the gravitational pull of sex.

And when it comes to the unconscious, we can only hope and pray that the limitations of sex provide a respite for this, too. Deep within everyone is a boiling, roiling, overflowing cauldron

93

of sexual emotions—longing, fear, guilt, anxiety, fantasy, pain, and happiness—and this constantly spills over into our lives, even parts that seem to have nothing to do with sex. It's the source of much positive energy (more about this later), but also the cause of much confusion and heartache. If the limitations of sex do nothing more than provide an occasional calming of this inner turmoil, they deserve hearty praise.

More Eros

There is another, more significant consolation: the limitations of sex enable us to become more, not less, erotic. This will take some explaining, I know.

The psychotherapist Rollo May, in his influential book *Love and Will*, has helped me understand that sex can actually be separated from eros; it can, moreover, be set *over against* eros: "We are in flight from eros—and we use sex as the vehicle for the flight. . . . We fly to *the sensation of sex in order to avoid the passion of eros.*"

Our culture proclaims loudly that anxiety about sex is archaic and encourages us to be free in our love. But May asks, "What of the *anxiety which comes precisely from this new freedom?*" The capacity for personal choice can create a heavy burden. Since nowadays everyone *ought* to feel free and uninhibited, anxiety has no way to act itself out externally, and thus it turns inward, inhibiting feelings and suffocating passion. Sex becomes a means of escaping the costly involvement of passion, a way to flee from the risks of total engagement with another. "We go to bed because we cannot hear each other; we go to bed because we are too shy to look in each other's eyes, and in bed one can turn away one's head."

May wants to broaden our understanding of eros. According to Greek mythology, Eros was the god who created life on earth. When the earth was barren, it was Eros who, with his

94

life-giving arrows, pierced the cold bosom of the earth—"an appealing symbolic picture of how Eros *incorporates* sex—those phallic arrows which pierce—as the instrument by which he creates life." Eros is the drive toward life, toward its expansion and fulfillment.

> Sex can be defined fairly adequately in physiological terms as consisting of the building up of bodily tensions and their release. Eros, in contrast, is the experiencing of the personal intentions and meaning of the act. . . . The end toward which sex points is gratification and relaxation, whereas eros is a desiring, longing, a forever reaching out, seeking to expand. . . . Eros is the drive toward union with what we belong to—union with our own possibilities, union with significant other persons in our world in relation to whom we discover our own self-fulfillment. Eros is the yearning in man which leads him to dedicate himself to seeking *arete*, the noble and good life.

Sexual intercourse is an intense experience of the union toward which eros pulls us, and thus we can easily understand how the two became closely linked. Sex is *the* act of procreation, *the* way we make life. But it can never completely satisfy the needs of eros. Eros longs for a more complete and lasting union, a far wider and higher expansion of life, than the joining of two bodies can offer. Sex, though, has the power to distract us, to deceive us into thinking we're satisfying our hunger for eros. This is why May says that sex can actually fight against eros. We can flee to sex in order to avoid the larger, riskier engagement of our whole being; we can use sex to escape authentic passion.

Perhaps, then, the limitations of sex are an opportunity to become more erotic in the larger sense. An eros freed from physical desire can help you rise toward a more fulfilled life and open you to receive a deeper passion. The very energy of sex, the power that pushes you toward union with another person, can pull you toward an intercourse with life itself, engaging not only your body but your mind and spirit as well.

Those who commit themselves to celibacy can be witnesses to the potential breadth of the truly erotic life. Thomas Moore, in *The Soul of Sex,* draws on his years as a Catholic monk to explain that celibacy does not mean being asexual:

> The soul of sex is not to be found only in the act of love but also in a life motivated by a broader love and extended pleasures. Living a full sensuous life with friends, intimates, and things, and indulging in pleasurable activities is an erotic life . . . . Sex finds natural expression in loving, passionate, active attention to the culture of one's own life and the culture of society. Sexual desire can be satisfied in creative engagement with the world, as long as desire, passion, pleasure, and other qualities of sex are brought into the enterprise.

Celibacy, then, can be a symbol for us: it reminds us that eros is not limited to genital sex, but can and must express itself in much broader ways. We could say that eros takes precedence over sex, the latter finding its deepest meaning and most intense pleasure only as nourished by the former. Eros makes sex sexy, in other words, but it can express itself in many ways. The absence of sex can be like the sudden narrowing of a riverbed, causing the mighty river of eros to flood its banks, covering the land with life-giving irrigation.

How easily you recognize this will depend on which side of satiation you're on. On the unsatisfied side, you're likely to think another sexual encounter will fulfill the longing; an actual woman or man, with a warm body and the promise of romance, will seem far more appealing than an abstract notion about "union with what we belong to." But on the satisfied side, when the driving force has been spent, you will inevitably come to a surprising and painful acknowledgment: the longing remains! After the afterglow, you will have the disconcerting

96

sensation of wanting . . . well, just more. The ground beneath your bed might have shaken and the fireworks exploded all around you, but in the morning the ground is still and the sky is gray. You will do your best not to notice this; you will try to dull the hunger pangs with new romantic thoughts and sexual fantasies, and for awhile this will help, but not forever. The pangs will get sharper until you have to admit you want something more, something far more satisfying. You might convince yourself that you simply need another person, thus purchasing a little more time in fantasyland. But sooner or later you will realize that you have in the center of your heart a black hole of fierce longing that sucks everything into it and is never satisfied. That's because you're an erotic person, a creature made for more than you now have, a creature who will not be happy with fleeting experiences of physical oneness, a creature who wants to—*needs to*—transcend your fragmentary life, a creature made in the image of God who will not be satisfied until you discover a more complete and lasting wholeness.

St. Augustine said that eros is the power that drives us to God. Only in God do we finally find a relationship that will heal our present brokenness. What you really want is not to satisfy lust but to become holy—whole—and that finally is found only in the Creator and Sustainer of the universe, the One who holds all things together in eternal unity. The wholeness you seek, as I said in the last chapter, is not the obliteration of self in divine union, but the fulfillment of self in an eternal communion, the completion of all you were meant to be in a fellowship with the One through whom you came into being.

The limitations of sex are sometimes difficult to endure. But their consolation can be a more erotic life—a life that embraces more of reality, a life of deeper passion, a life that intensifies our longing and lifts it toward the Divine Lover who alone can satisfy it.

10

Mind If I Lean on Your Arm?

The Limitations of Confidence

Near the top of everyone's list of Great American Virtues is confidence. We prize the willingness to take on a challenge and get the job done; we applaud those who not only play with the band but have the chops to perform their own solos.

Not everyone has the self-assurance of an Albert Einstein, who, when asked what he would have said had there been no confirmation of his general theory of relativity, replied, "I would have been obliged to pity our dear God. The theory is correct." But we admire this spirit! Give us a person with moxie, with mettle, with the never-say-uncle stamina to persevere against all odds! Give us a Robert Fitzsimmons, who said of his boxing opponents, "The bigger they are, the harder they fall." Give us a Samuel Goldwyn, who refused to change his mind about a particular script, saying, "I am willing to admit that I may not always be right, but I am never wrong." Crazy as it seems, we know what he means.

When my daughters were young, they would insist, "I can do it myself, Daddy!" Even if I had doubts, I was always proud of them; I wanted them to believe in themselves, to have the self-esteem necessary to assume they could do difficult things. Confidence, I knew, could take them a long way down the road of achievement.

My own experience had proven this. In my first year of college, I saw myself as a B student, and, sure enough, that's what I was. But during the second quarter of my sophomore year, I surprised myself by earning more As than Bs. It was an accident, but nonetheless I gave it a harder push the next quarter and came up with all As. From then on, my self-image changed: I was now an A student, and for the rest of my educational career—through college and graduate school—that's what I received. I began every class wondering who the *other* A students would be. Once during graduate school I received a B, contrary to The Way It Was Supposed to Be, and I argued with the professor until he raised my grade (confidence, I should mention, can be a pain in the backside of others).

We all have stories similar to this, if not about grades, then about athletic feats or sales quotas or dating adventures or some other enterprise. We *believe* in confidence, don't we?

Crushed Confidence

But what happens when our confidence gets crushed flatter than a laptop computer, flatter, even, than the microchips in it? This happens most often through failure, I suppose, or, more accurately, by what we perceive as failure: you stand up to a bully but get beat up; you take a difficult class but flunk; you bring home a trophy but it isn't shiny enough to win parental praise; you audition for a play but aren't called back; you submit a manuscript for publication but get enough rejection slips to wallpaper your bedroom; you pour thirty years into your company but are forced into early retirement; you give yourself to your spouse but he walks out on you. Many are the ways your ego can take a beating, and, each time, your confidence is undermined. If you step up to the plate, ready to knock a home run, but a ninety-mile-per-hour fastball hits you in the head, you'll be nervous the next time at bat; if it happens again, you'll dread your place in the lineup; if it happens yet again, you'll want to quit the game altogether.

I've experienced this, too. The boy who made all As had enough confidence to become a pastor and lead a congregation; some failures and embarrassments along the way humbled him but didn't seriously shake his confidence. When he began work as a seminary president, he had enough confidence to assume the challenge with energy and optimism. Each success bolstered his self-assurance; each triumph emboldened him and helped him believe he could do the job well. But one day a failure in his past caught up with him and put the trustees in a bind, with the result that he was asked to resign. Shame, guilt, hurt, anger—every negative emotion you can think of—pummeled his confidence into a bloody mess, leaving it unconscious with barely a pulse. The man who, a few months before, thought nothing of speaking to thousands of people, was suddenly nervous about walking into a bookstore or asking for help at the bank.

I know something about the limitations of confidence, and one of the things I learned is that they leave you in a very dangerous place.

The Birth of Courage

The limitations of confidence bring you to a fork in the road and force you to make a choice filled with enormous significance. You can either go down the road of increasing fear or down the road of renewed courage.

The easiest direction to take, and thus the most tempting, is to avoid further failure. This leads to withdrawal and resignation. If your confidence is lost, it seems safer not to risk anymore; if your self-esteem is bruised, it seems better not to get back in the ring where you will surely be punched, maybe even knocked out. The instinct to protect yourself is so basic, so primitive, that it's extremely difficult not to take this road when you're unsure of yourself. And the farther you travel along it, the harder it is to turn around.

The other direction is both more difficult and more life-renewing. It's frightening beyond description, but it's the only real option for anyone who wants to grow as a person: you go forward anyway. Your confidence may be no larger than a gnat's eyelash, but you try it again, you risk yet more failure, you let fear issue its dire warnings, but for some reason, not fully understood even by yourself, you ignore them and just keep going. When that happens, the driving energy of your life shifts from confidence to courage.

This is the first great consolation of stumbling confidence: it offers the opportunity to become a courageous person. When you face a difficult challenge, one you're not certain you can handle, one that twists your stomach into knots and turns your knees into Jello, what do you do? You pull up your pantyhose or straighten your tie and give it another try. You let a bucket down into a well you had thought was dry and you pull up something you didn't know was there.

Courage is a mysterious virtue. At first it operates on its own, pushing you to step up to the plate one more time to wait for the pitch—and you do it, contrary to logic, contrary to expectations, contrary to every instinct within you. Naked courage, alone and shivering with terror, drives you. But courage is not the loner it seems; it's really gregarious, prodigal in its solicitations for company. So, eventually something sidles up to courage—a newfound strength, maybe, or a different perspective, or a new skill—and perhaps something else joins them, and before you know it, you have become a larger person able to meet a larger challenge.

During the summers of my college years, I painted the exterior of houses. I did it for one reason: money. My friends were camp counselors and lifeguards, but I needed more money than fun employment could provide. So after graduating from high school, without having so much as painted a single board in my entire life, I formed a painting company and advertised in the local newspaper. How hard could it be? I had watched commercials on television, after all, memorizing what they had said about the advantages of latex over oil-based paint ("latex expands and breathes . . . ," etc.), and that helped me bluff my way through my first conversation with a prospective client. After walking around the house several times, I pulled an estimate out of the absolute vacuum of my ignorance, and for reasons known only to God, I got the job.

That left only one problem. I had to paint the house. Which meant climbing ladders, a fact I never really thought about until I pulled into the driveway of the large colonial house with about twelve thousand little windowpanes reaching to the heavens.

I hate heights. I'm not afraid of airplanes or tall buildings, but don't ask me to walk along a ledge or climb a ladder. This is something I should have taken into account before forming my company, I know, but I lay the blame on my financial despera-tion. So there I was, looking up the side of the house, and the eaves were so high I nearly got a nosebleed just *thinking* about being at that altitude. It scared the turpentine out of me. The first time I extended the ladder to reach the second story, a herd of butterflies stirred up a hurricane in my stomach—and that was before I took my first step up. By the third, I was wonder-ing how you back out of a painting contract, and by the tenth, I would have started crying if I hadn't been afraid of the shaking it would have caused.

It was going to be a hellish summer. If my confidence had been buried any deeper it would have emerged on the streets of Shanghai. But I was desperate, and I had no other job possibilities, so I kept going up the ladder. At the time, I wouldn't have dignified my resolve by calling it "courage"; it seemed more like craziness, like something that should get me committed to a mental institution. But I kept doing it, day by day, month by month, until, by the end of the summer, I had painted about a dozen houses and made enough money for my first year of college. I can't say I ever became comfortable on the ladder, but I got better at it. By forcing myself to do it, I learned *how* to do it—how to focus on the painting and not the potential falling, how to balance myself, how to lean out without jiggling the ladder, and, most of all, how to grit my teeth and keep doing something I *really* didn't want to do.

The loss of confidence can force you to rely on courage, and courage brings with it new skills and virtues.

Leaning on Others

Another consolation that often comes with the limitations of confidence is a new relationship with others. When we're not sure of ourselves, and we want to keep facing challenges, we have to lean on steadier arms. Confidence in our own abilities isolates us, leaves us voluntarily marooned on an island of self-sufficiency. When we lose it, we're dragged out of our egocentricity, often unwillingly, and to our surprise we discover the joy of being part of a community.

After my first year in seminary, I became the summer pastor of a Congregational church in eastern Washington. I was overflowing with enthusiasm for the opportunity, full of beans and the love of God and certain I could handle anything that came my way. Ignorance can instill a lively recklessness.

Things went so well in the first few weeks that I wasn't even worried when I received a call asking if I would conduct a funeral. This was not unlike asking a first-year medical student to perform an appendectomy, but I was too excited at the prospect to understand my peril. This became clearer when I sat in the living room of the grieving widow, and I asked how her husband had passed away. "Well," she responded, "we had had an argument, and my husband walked into the room and said, 'Watch this,' as he put a gun to his head and pulled the trigger."

I suddenly felt that I had a gun at my own head. What could I possibly say at that moment, and, for *God's* sake, at the funeral? How could I plan a service under these circumstances? Who was I to think I could be a pastoral bulwark against the tsunami of anger and grief that was crashing down upon that family?

About an hour later, when I was back in my office, I found a telephone book and looked up the number of the local Presbyterian church. When Pastor Ted answered I blurted out my despair: "I need help! I don't know what I'm doing!"

"Why don't you come over," he said.

So the rest of the day he let me unload my fears, and we discussed the purpose of a funeral and what I should expect at the service. "By the way," he said, "which mortuary is dealing with this?"

When I told him, he put his head in his hand and said, "Oh oh."

That was roughly equivalent to hearing a surgeon saying, "Oops." "What do you mean?" I asked. "Is that a problem?"

"Big problem. It's the mortician. Nice guy, but a boozer. Always drunk. I've had services with him at ten in the morning and he was too drunk to drive. Where will the burial be?"

"Walla Walla."

"Oh boy. That's thirty miles away, and you have to take a twisting mountain road to get there. And you will be expected to ride in the hearse, of course."

I was drowning in fear, going down for the third time, and Ted could see it in my eyes. So he threw me the lifeline of his experience. Over the next couple of days he lent me books, helped me plan the service, coached me on how to keep an eye on the mortician, especially while standing at the graveside (Ted's theory was that he had a bottle hidden under the fender of the hearse from which he took swigs while the mourners were praying), and walked me through a likely scenario of what would happen. I was still afraid, but I wasn't alone. He bolstered my courage enough to get me through my first funeral. I don't remember much of what he said, but I still recall with vivid clarity the sun shining through Ted's sandy hair as he put his comforting hand on my shoulder.

That came to mind when, a couple of years ago, Ted telephoned to say hello. By then I had conducted many, many funerals and was leading a seminary that helped prepare students for their own ministries. We reminisced and laughed about what was not at all funny at the time, and though we had not spoken for twenty-five years, I felt a lasting bond with him. My loss of confidence had forced me to reach out, and the hand that reached back assured me I was not alone.

Help!

What I did between talking with Ted and appearing at the mortuary was pray. I had prayed before, certainly, but now I *prayed*. I asked for help as though my life depended on it; I flung myself at the door of heaven, banging on it until my knuckles were raw; I pleaded with the Almighty to save me from the follies of my premature and wholly unreasonable confidence; I sat on the corner with my little tin cup begging for a handout. There's nothing like terror to boost one's spiritual fervor.

And this is the best consolation of all: when you come to the limitations of confidence, you have to throw yourself in the arms of God—and you have good reason to hope you will be caught and held. For the God of the Bible has a definite preference for people who know they're in over their heads and don't know the first thing about treading water.

Which brings to mind one of my favorite New Testament stories. The disciples of Jesus were crossing the Sea of Galilee. It had been a tough night for sailing, with a hard wind against them and mean waves pounding their bow. But the storm wasn't half as frightening as what happened next: Jesus showed up, walking on the water. I can't say they were scared out of their minds, because they thought they had seen a ghost, a response that seems to me entirely reasonable, given the circumstances. If they weren't out of their minds, though, they must have been close to it, and when they heard what Jesus said—"Take heart, it is I; do not be afraid"—that might have been enough to push some of them over the edge.

The edge Peter went over was the side of the boat. With the impulsive bravado for which he became famous, he said, "Lord, if it is you, command me to come to you on the water." Since these words came from Peter, it's not clear whether they reveal a confidence in Jesus or a confidence that if Jesus could do it, so could he. The Gospels give the impression that Peter was the sort of guy who elicited more than his share of rolled eyes and knowing looks when he wasn't around to see them.

One of the lessons in this story, perhaps, is that you should be careful about what you ask of Jesus. Sometimes he grants your request. "Come," he said, leaving Peter little choice but to go. So over the edge he went and across the waves, as though he knew what he was doing, as though it were the most natural thing in the world for a man to be walking on a stormy sea in the middle of the night toward what a few minutes earlier he had thought was a ghost. At some point, he came to his senses. Matthew says simply, "But when he noticed the strong wind, he became frightened." Well, no doubt. He was frightened in the way that a man is frightened when he sees his life coming to an end, when he knows he has just done something really stupid, when he knows there's no way out of the dangerous circumstances he has gotten himself into, when he has lost whatever confidence he once had, when he feels himself sinking down into the depths faster than a lead weight.

"Lord, save me!" he cried out, and that was the smartest thing he did all evening. Prayer doesn't get any more basic than this; prayer stripped of flowery language and lofty sentiments and liturgical correctness comes down to this: *Help!* And Jesus, once again, granted his request, reaching out his hand to catch him before he went all the way down.

As a fisherman Peter had spent many a night on the water, and I would guess that when storms had assailed him he had done plenty of both cursing and praying, and he probably had many stories, mostly true, to tell his comrades in the warmth of a fire and a stiff drink. But never had he had a night like that one, with his confidence sinking and the threat of drowning lapping at his feet and Jesus reaching out to pull him out of the water.

Later, after Jesus had been killed on a Roman cross and raised to life by a God who makes all things new, a God who brings triumph out of tragedy, Jesus appointed Saul of Tarsus to be his witness to the Gentiles. But if it weren't for the honor of the thing, there were more than a few times Paul would have just as soon retired to a seaside villa. It could get nasty witnessing to Jesus. About one trip into Asia he said, "We were so utterly, unbearably crushed that we despaired of life itself. Indeed, we felt that we had received the sentence of death so that we would rely not on ourselves but on God who raises the dead."

107

The sentence of death is about as low as you can get. Those in the grave are utterly, absolutely helpless; they don't have much confidence. Not able to rely on themselves, they have to rely on God who raises the dead.

That's the great consolation of the limitations of confidence. They leave no choice but to rely on God who delights in helping those without the wherewithal to help themselves.

11

Ignoring the Reviews

The Limitations of Public Approval

I will never forget the first time I heard Darrell Gardner play the trumpet. His father was a traveling evangelist who visited my father's congregation to hold "special meetings." As an added attraction, Darrell played a solo each night before his father preached. The warm-up act, in my judgment, was hotter than the main event. Flaming hair swept back, legs set apart, and back arched, Darrell put the shiny gold instrument to his lips and blew like Gabriel announcing the End of the Age. He slid up and down the scales, catapulting from the basement into the stratosphere, careening from *pianissimo* to *fortissimo,* trilling and glissading and flourishing his way through old hymns and gospel songs. The congregation was awed by his prodigious skill, and I was beyond awe: I was transfixed, overcome. Those were the days before you applauded in church, which was just as well, because I was too paralyzed to move my hands.

At that moment, two things happened: Darrell Gardner became my hero and I determined to be like him. I was going to blow the horn so that I, too, could stand in front of an audience and dazzle them with my skill. This resolve took place when I was in the fourth grade, just as my school was offering music lessons for interested students. My parents bought me a trumpet, and I started lessons and buzzed my lips raw.

Not long after I began, the Gardners visited our home. When someone mentioned that I was now studying the trumpet, Darrell graciously asked me to play. So I blew my heart out for him (I was not lacking in the confidence we considered in the last chapter). When I finished, he patted me on the back, enthusiastically praising my rendition of "Twinkle, Twinkle, Little Star."

My hero's approval energized me. I practiced all the harder, determined to play my own solos. Eventually I did, and though I was never as accomplished as Darrell, I was pretty good, good enough to earn a seat in citywide orchestras, even winning a few musical contests along the way. For some reason, during my sophomore year in college, I abruptly quit. I'm not sure why I did this, especially after all the time I had invested in acquiring the skill, but I'm sure those years of doing something well and receiving affirmation from others were important in the development of my personality.

We all want—and need, especially in our early years—the audience's approval. Esteem from other people is a crucial building block of the esteem we have for ourselves. As early as 1902, sociologist C. H. Cooley introduced the idea of the looking-glass self: our self-understanding is based on our perception of others' perception of us. Little was done with this idea until the middle of the century, when psychoanalytic theories began to stress the role of interpersonal relationships in shaping personality. Since then, a growing body of research has left little doubt that we see ourselves reflected in the response of others. Most important are our parents; they must communicate acceptance, through affectionate touch and affirming talk, for us to develop a healthy self-regard. Other relationships are also important. Extended family members, teachers, coaches, and peers play a significant role in the formation of self-image. When we receive approval we feel worthy and deserving of our place in the world; when that approval is not forthcoming, we are prone to devalue ourselves and carry a load of shame.

Addiction

As is often the case, however, something necessary for health can, when exceeding its bounds, become destructive. Affirmation, so necessary in our early years, can turn into an addiction that stunts psychological growth. Well-known lines from Ecclesiastes come to mind: "For everything there is a season, and a time for every matter under heaven." At the beginning of our lives, others help build self-respect at the core of our beings, and this, in turn, enables us to become our truest selves—to individuate, as psychologists say. As we enter adulthood we should be growing in psychological independence, learning to be faithful to our own convictions about who we are and who we want to be—regardless of what others think of us.

But it's not that simple! Affirmation is too addictive. We easily become dependent on it because of intractable fears. Recall again our discussion of Ernest Becker. Our deepest terror, he tells us, is death. At an early age we sense our vulnerability in a threatening universe. So we invest our parents—and ultimately others—with power to save us. Not able to defeat death ourselves, we project our hopes on stand-in heroes, on those we think (unconsciously) can shield us. And then, if they smile back at us, acknowledging and affirming us—well, it's a powerful shot of a potent drug that goes straight into the bloodstream. Someone we value values us; the one we had looked to for salvation embraces us; our god has smiled on us, and thus we must be secure. In the alchemy of the unconscious this affirmation turns into proof of our own worth. Now we share the heroics of our hero!

So it's hard to break the habit; we're not easily released from addiction to approval. Praise is like morphine, a drug that has been administered to me in three different emergency rooms, and, I must say, I've grown quite fond of it. When a kidney stone slices its way down your urethra, or your arm snaps in two, or your shoulder rips apart, it's a fine thing to have, something you want the nurse to keep pumping into your body with as big a syringe as she can find. Once, when I was telling the nurse I thought she was the most wonderful person in all the world and begging her to stay by my side forever, she told me she wasn't fooled: I had fallen in love with her morphine. Perhaps to dampen my ardor, she gave me a medical lecture, telling me that morphine doesn't take away pain but works magic in the brain so you don't care anymore. As she explained this I became aware that, sure enough, my pain was still there, but hey! So what? I had no time to fret over sad matters! I was too busy thinking up my next joke, too busy having a wonderful time basking in her attention.

Public approval works in a similar way. It doesn't remove the terror of death; it does, however, distract us from it, at least for awhile. It plays a trick with our minds, making us think we're more worthwhile, more valuable, and hence more secure. On another level of awareness, we know this is nonsense, but we don't care. It feels so good, so *believable* in the manner of a good book or movie, that it allows us to escape.

Try this: recall your most common daydreams. How many of your fantasies have to do with winning the praise of others? How many are about getting the recognition you deserve, receiving the gratitude of others, attaining the public's applause, basking in the affections of those most important to you?

For many years I made my living in an extremely danger-ous occupation: I was a preacher. No one is more susceptible

112

to the seductions of public praise, with the possible exception of politicians and movie stars. To be at the center of a community's attention and to receive nearly constant affirmation about your wisdom and compassion and inspiration is a heady experience. Because you're engaged in spiritual ministry, doing God's work, really *wanting* to glorify God, it's easy to overlook the ordinary psychological dynamics in play. As the leader, you have received the projected hopes of the folks in the congregation; you have been set up on a pedestal, their hero. They are using you, to be sure, but you are using them, too, allowing them to feed your hunger for approval. As one of my pastor friends puts it, it's easy to start believing your own press releases. Before you know it, you become dependent on being liked, dependent on wowing the congregation Sunday by Sunday.

One of the lowest moments of my life—this is painful to confess, but it makes the point—was after a particular Sunday worship service. Instead of going immediately to the door to greet the worshipers and, not incidentally, to hear their responses to my sermon, I went first to the bathroom. As I stood with my unzipped robe billowing at my sides like black wings, doing what men do with their faces to the wall, another fellow came into the restroom to attend to his own business. We said hello to each other, and then I waited. I expected to hear from him something like, "Great sermon, pastor!" or maybe, "You were terrific today!" But I heard nothing. So I kept waiting, prolonging my activities, taking my time, worrying that his silence indicated he thought my sermon was bad, worrying that maybe this was just the beginning of a bad-response Sunday. Then I suddenly became aware of my pathetic behavior, and, given the context of this revelation, I felt like a needy little pervert, a despicable sicko. I wanted to hang my head in shame and leave the sanctuary immediately. But of course I went to the door to receive whatever praise might be thrown my way. I was like a

113

wino, disgusted with himself but thirsty enough to retrieve a bottle from the gutter to drain its last few drops.

Withdrawal

The affirmation of others is like a drug that elevates the spirit, boosts confidence, and deceives us into believing we might prevail against things that threaten us. But what goes up, as they say, must come down. There must inevitably come a time when reviews turn negative, maybe even nasty.

This can happen in a variety of ways. It can happen when we're in the wrong; we receive a reprimand because we haven't performed adequately at work, perhaps, or we cause a scene with our anger, or we get caught in a moral indiscretion. It can happen when we're in the right; we stand on principle, argue for a course of action we believe to be best, but we're alone in our convictions (think of Winston Churchill, despised for years because of his insistence on the Nazi threat). It can happen because of human fickleness; what's good today can be bad tomorrow (think of Jesus Christ, who just a few days after hearing the crowds say, "Crown him!" heard them say, "Crucify him!"). It can happen because we quit trying to please others; for once we decide to do what we want, what will make us happy (think of yourself, the first time you did something as an adult that seriously displeased your parents).

Whatever brave front you put up when you arrive at the limitations of public approval, you have to be frightened. Even the person who seems the freest spirit in the universe, I suspect, bears a quiet pain when applause stops and criticism starts. Withdrawal is never easy. Without *someone* offering approval, you're left alone, dangling by yourself over the abyss. The possibilities are frightening: you could be wrong, you could be mistaken, you could be stupid, you could be unlikable, you

114

could be unworthy, you could be, God forbid, unsafe in a very dangerous world.

Insight

The first blessing this confers is insight: losing the approval of the public can free us from a narrow focus and enable us to see a larger view of reality. This might seem a dubious advantage, for what we will see is the vanity around us, the emptiness of much that passes for human life.

Recall, for example, the last time you got ready for a party. Remember how you worried about what to wear (would it be appropriate for the occasion?), and whether you should have had your hair done differently (is anyone still wearing it this sculpted?), and whether your shoes looked like they had come off the bargain racks at K-Mart (are they just too *last year*?). And then, when you got to the party, remember how you quickly scanned the room to see what everyone was wearing (whew! two others in jeans), and you felt something itchy in your nose and panicked that something gross might be hanging out of it (he's staring at my nose, I can tell), and how in conversations you heard, at best, 15 percent of what others were saying because you were coming up with witty responses (as soon as he shuts up I'll tell that funny story).

Now—this is the important part—*imagine everyone else doing the same thing!* If you can picture this, even for a moment, you suddenly see the immense absurdity of it all. We're worried about what people think of us, but people aren't thinking about us at all, except to worry about what we're thinking of them. No one has the time to approve or disapprove of us, for they're too preoccupied with their own quest for acceptance.

Here's the irony of the situation: we're actually put off by those who work hard at winning us to their side. People who seem most intent on impressing us are those who inspire the urge to freshen a drink or visit the powder room or change the oil in the car. There's something unappealing about anyone who is put together too carefully, who has polished the sheen on self-presentation to a high gloss. Which may be why my friends tease me about my hair. It always looks nice (humbly speaking). I can go six weeks without a haircut and drive around all day in my convertible, and it still looks well-groomed. You might not consider this a serious problem, and I would agree it's not on the same level with starvation in Africa or war with Iraq. But my friends give me a hard time about this. Lately, I've gotten sensitive enough about this that I've begun running my fingers through my hair before a party, trying to give myself a messier style. I've even considered getting it spiked. But that would really set them off, as it would me if they did it, because we all dislike someone who breaks too much of a sweat over being liked, who is too eager for our admiration, who monitors our every response, who is like a needy dog waiting for a pat on the head.

A few years ago a seminary student decided I was The Best Preacher in the World. He drove two hours every Sunday to my church, taking notes, making appointments to discuss the science and art of public persuasion, begging me to listen to tapes of his own sermons. After awhile, it annoyed me. He was following too close to my heels, and I admit the recurring urge to turn around and give him a hard kick.

But isn't there something attractive about a person secure enough not to care about the reaction of others? Someone un-afraid to be his or her unique self? The reason we find this appealing, I think, is because we admire the inner freedom this requires; we would like to be liberated from our own fear of disapproval. So we're encouraged by those who don't seem to care what anyone thinks, who have the courage to act out of the integrity of who they really are.

So if the limitations of public approval offer us even a brief insight into the games we play, they deserve our gratitude. It may be disheartening to see the meaningless nonsense that goes on around us and within us, but it's also liberating. It might even provide some encouragement to be ourselves.

At Last, Ourselves

To be ourselves. To be the unique individuals God intended— that's what we need and, in a deep place of longing beyond the reach of articulate expression, what we want. The limitations of public approval present us with the opportunity to do this, and it's their chief consolation.

"For everything there is a season . . ." In the spring and summer of our lives we need affirmation shining on us, nurturing us into growth. But in autumn and winter, when the sun slants and shortens and steals into seclusion, we must rise to the warmth of a benevolent light within ourselves. In our middle years, God granting us courage, we enter a season of integration when we take joys and sorrows, achievements and failures, light and shadows, and, God granting grace, discover a balance that gives birth to an independent and more complete self.

Unlike the passing of seasons, this doesn't happen automatically (metaphors, too, have limitations), and it certainly doesn't happen without the pain of owning the difficult limitations we have been considering in this book. But it can happen, has been known to happen to many people, and it can happen for us, too, if we seize the opportunities that make it possible.

These opportunities, I'm sorry to say, usually come with considerable pain. They tend to conceal themselves in difficult, stressful circumstances; they like to hide in episodes that strip away our most cherished securities.

For me this happened most dramatically in the loss of a professional position, something I've already mentioned. During my first year of exile, I wrote a book that chronicled the despair and hope that contended for my soul. Now, a year and a half after I finished that manuscript, the passage of time has put some things in a brighter light, things I could not see in the dark, disorienting fog of my emotions. One of the most important gifts that came my way in those days of misery, I now realize, was the loss of public approval. I was kicked off the pedestal in many minds, and almost overnight I went from admired hero to despised bum. This was awful, almost beyond enduring; there were days I felt as though I had died. But in truth, it was a valuable gift, one of the most important I have received. It forcibly separated me—the *essential* me—from the public's perception of me. Without an audience affirming me into being, who was I? After being stripped of my image, I wrapped myself in that question. Who am I, apart from praise and blame? Who am I, apart from admiring and condemning crowds? Who am I, apart from what I had seen reflected in the mirror of others' perceptions?

An answer began to emerge from those question-filled days, and I began to feel a new freedom and power—freedom because I was being liberated from worry about my image, and power because my self was being transformed from one that weakly clung to the whims of others to one that stands steady on the foundation of authentic identity. To learn, not just in my head but in the depths of my being, that I was someone different from and always more than the perception of others was like being in a hot, stuffy room and having the windows thrown open. To use another metaphor, it was like being falsely sentenced to prison and having the cell doors thrown open after an overturned conviction. I can't say I'm now *completely* immune to the judgments of others (I'm still learning how to put all this in practice); most of the time, though, I'm not much impressed with the cheering or overly worried about the jeering. I am who I am, thank God. And yes, *thank God,* because who I am is a child of God, a beloved of God, a man in whom God takes delight. I had known this before, to be sure, but I didn't know how much

I still needed to learn it until I came to the limitations of public approval. Enduring these limitations was something I wouldn't have wished on my worst enemy; now it's something that, if not for the dishonor of it, I would covet for my dearest friends.

This, then, is my witness: when I lost the praise of the public, I gained knowledge of myself, and I testify to this in the confidence that you may well experience the same.

12

A Sudden Interest in the Future of Social Security

The Limitations of Money

Let's begin with an affirmation so obvious it shouldn't need to be mentioned. But because you know I spent part of my life in a line of work notorious for harping on the evils of materialism, let me be clear: money is good. It may not be the highest good (no one would say that), but it's high enough to command much of our time and passion. It provides nothing less than physical existence, enabling us to purchase food, clothing, and shelter. With these, we buy security itself, or at least a way around the more dramatic causes of insecurity.

In addition, money makes possible much that elevates life above mere survival: education, entertainment, arts, scientific research, religious communities—most worthy endeavors rest on a financial base. Money rounds us out and empowers us to embody our values in this world. When you write a check for Habitat for Humanity or the American Cancer Society, you commit part of yourself to housing the poor or finding a cure for cancer.

Even when money seems to buy nothing more than pleasure, the pleasure we choose manifests our personalities. For example, consider an object that is most often an unnecessary luxury—a sailboat. Owning one, it has been said, is like owning a hole in the water into which you pour money. This cliché is especially annoying when it comes out of the mouth of your spouse, because it's true. For several years I owned a twenty-seven-foot sailboat, the *Jennifer Lee*, and though I didn't spend as much on her as on my daughter for whom she was named, it was probably close. Berthing, insurance, repairs—don't get me started. Which is why another cliché came into being: the two happiest days in a boat owner's life are the day he buys a boat and the day he sells it. But for me, this one was not true. The day I sold my boat was very sad, indeed, and would have been even if I hadn't accidentally sold it to two different buyers and nearly gotten sued. We had had great times together, *Jennifer Lee* and I—times of laugh-out-loud exuberance and white-knuckle terror that will forever be fixed in my memory. I was able to enjoy my love of the sea and to share it with my friends. The modest craft became a kind of extension of myself. Accordingly, I cared for it with meticulous concern: I washed and waxed it, repaired its nicks, and oiled its teak; I even bought a set of tools to work on the engine, though I didn't know a diesel from a weasel. The only tool I actually used was a large wrench, which I used to bang the daylights out of the fuel pump when the engine sputtered, but I intended to learn more, to rise above my historic aversion to mechanical matters, so I studied manu-

121

als on winter evenings when I wasn't poring over navigational charts or thumbing through sailing magazines.

Owning a boat is not necessary, strictly speaking; you can argue that there are better ways to spend money. That boat, though, enriched my life in meaningful, even healing ways. It was an escape from stress , and, perhaps more importantly, it provided a constant, uncomplicated delight, an almost pure, childlike love. Sure, the money might have been given to the poor, but I know I would have been poorer for it, and not just financially.

So I'm a believer in money. It keeps us alive, allows us to develop as persons, and opens doors to many pleasures.

Never Enough

But money has its limitations, the chief being that it runs out too soon for most of us. We may enjoy gourmet repasts and designer clothes and million-dollar mansions, but do we ever satisfy our other needs? Do we ever express our values as fully as we would like? Does our quest to explore and experience this world ever come to an end? And—this is the most important question—do we ever spend enough to feel secure? If our most troubling anxiety is vulnerability in a dangerous world—death!—no amount of money, however vast, can deliver us from it, and, strangely, this very failure increases our desire for more. If only we had another twenty thousand to pay off debts. If only we had a bigger home. If only we had a more secure retirement fund. If only the stock market would turn around. If only we won the lottery. Each "if only" relentlessly leads to the next, because desire never finds satiation, the driving momentum of our lives never finds a resting place. There are some things money can't buy.

The limitations of money become evident when bills pile high and bank accounts run low, and they become *mercilessly* evident when we have plenty to spend but nothing to buy that can satisfy us.

A Deadly Embrace

These limitations put us in a highly dangerous situation. They can, and often do, lead to greater preoccupation with money, to the strengthening of money's grip on our lives. Or they can lead to the undermining, perhaps even the final breaking, of money's power.

Money is a power. I do not mean simply that those who possess it can accumulate what they want and do as they please, though in one sense this is true. I mean something more fundamental: money itself is power. Money has an authority that exceeds what currency and coins do for us; it has spiritual sway. Jesus referred to it as Mammon, a Semitic name. He personalized it. This was not a common practice in his day; there are no parallel references in historical texts. It was as though he wanted to stress that money is not simply an object; it is a living, personal force. "You cannot serve God and Mammon," he said, and putting it that way, he lifted Mammon to the status of a rival god. Take your choice, but be careful: you gotta dance with them that brung ya, and it could be difficult to leave the party.

Was there ever a culture more in thrall to Mammon than our own? Capitalism brings many blessings, we all acknowledge, but at a price we would be fools to ignore: it depends on an aggressive, expansive consumerism that reaches into almost every corner of every day. We attend to reports from Wall Street as though monitoring vital signs in an intensive care unit, growing especially anxious if there is any drop in consumer confidence. Life in modern America depends on selling and buying, and then *more* selling and buying . . . of what? Some years ago Robert Maynard Hutchinson said it well: "Our real problems are concealed from us by our current remarkable prosperity which results in part from our production of arms, which we do not expect to use, and in part from our new way of getting rich, which is to buy things from one another that we do not want, at prices we cannot pay, on terms we cannot meet, because of advertising we do not believe." To bring this up to date, we should add, "on the Internet we do not understand."

I'm not knocking capitalism. I'm only making the point that the economic system that has served us well and we are eager to export to the rest of the world has a price, part of which is having to dance with Mammon, a partner whose embrace is not easily broken.

In Victor Hugo's novel *The Toilers of the Sea,* a character named Claubert wishes to rob a shipload of people. He steers the ship onto a sandbar and, attempting to appear very noble, puts everyone in a lifeboat and sends them off to an island where he says they will be saved. He remains behind, pretending to be a hero. As soon as they're out of sight, he goes through the staterooms and safes on the ship, gathering all the money and putting it on his person. He plans to leap off and swim a short distance to a nearby island by which ships regularly pass. He will be rescued with all the money, while the other passengers will be lost.

Loaded with cash, he leaps over the side of the ship, cuts through the surface of the water, goes down, touches the bottom, and then pushes off, surging upward to the surface. But then something grabs him. It's a giant octopus. Icy tentacles wrap around him, and he struggles to escape its cold embrace. But even as he tears himself away from one tentacle, another grabs him, until they clutch his neck, his waist, and his legs, and pull him to his death.

When we cling to money, something bigger than we could have imagined takes hold of us. It is Mammon, the spirit of materialism, and its embrace is deadly. Most often, it destroys by distorting our perspective.

124

About a dozen years ago a friend of mine, a real estate agent, facilitated the sale of a home, in which one rich old man paid another rich old man $900,000 cash. But the deal nearly fell through because they spent three days arguing about six potted plants. My friend said it was difficult to be in the middle of this, especially when she thought of her twenty-year-old daughter fighting a losing battle against Hodgkin's disease.

Something more was at stake than the value of six potted plants. Though only worth a few dollars, they had become symbols, as material objects do. Mammon so distorts our perspective that we cling to things and money, not for the needs of existence, not for the growth of our humanity, not even for the enjoyment of luxury, but ultimately to affirm our worth. The longer it takes to count our possessions, the easier it is to believe that we ourselves count, that we ourselves have value. So two old rich guys had to hang on to every potted plant, had to win, because in losing even a single one they might lose part of themselves.

Lessons from a Fool

This power of Mammon to skew our values was no doubt why Jesus said, "Take care! Be on your guard against all kinds of greed; for one's life does not consist in the abundance of possessions." He issued this warning after being asked to play a parental role between two fighting brothers. "Teacher," one of them said, "tell my brother to divide the family inheritance with me." The younger one was speaking, I would guess, unhappy that according to Jewish law his elder brother received double his own share, or perhaps he was still waiting to see his measly one-third of the estate. Squabbles over money can bring out the worst in sibling relationships, as many discover. He was saying, "Help me out here, Jesus! Everyone knows you stand for what's good and fair. Tell my brother to shape up and hand over my share!"

So Jesus cautioned against "all kinds of greed"—legal and illegal, moral and immoral. Greed is greed, and mighty dangerous. To illustrate his point, Jesus told a story about a successful farmer. Year after year his fields produced bumper crops, until his barns were so full they couldn't take another kernel of grain. What would he do? He would expand, of course! He would tear down his barns and build bigger ones, because as everyone knows, bigger is better. Yes, he said, I will erect storehouses that will be the talk of the region, storehouses like no one has ever seen, and I'll fill them, yes I will, and you can bet your last sack of grain on it. And then I will say to my soul, "Soul, you have ample goods laid up for many years; relax, eat, drink, be merry."

He was the sort of guy who, in our era, would be named alumnus of the year by his alma mater, and featured on the cover of *Forbes*, and invited to lecture MBA students on economies of scale and the future of agribusiness, and called to testify before the Senate Committee on Agriculture. In no time he would have a best-seller on the front table at Barnes and Noble entitled, *Seven Steps to Stuffed Silos—How You, Too, Can Liberate Your Inner Farmer.* Many of us would buy it, too, because we like to learn from successful people, from those who know how to set goals and reach them, from those who know how to profit from strategic planning and hard work.

But God called him a fool. That's how Jesus ended his story: "God said to him, 'You fool! This very night your life is being demanded of you. And the things you have prepared, whose will they be?' So it is with those who store up treasures for themselves but are not rich toward God."

Just as we've picked up the farmer's book and are reading the blurbs on the back, we hear a deep, resonant voice, filled with the wisdom of eternity, and it says, "Save your money; he's a fool."

How could this be? The man embodies so much of what we admire in this country, doesn't he? How can you fault him? How can *God* fault him?

He was a fool, I think, because *he confused the means of life with the end of life.* He allowed the means by which he lived to become the end for which he lived. He crossed over the line from living *by* his wealth to living *for* his wealth. Productive fields, surplus crops, large barns, good investments—nothing wrong with these things, provided they lead toward more important ends. But here's a rule: means always try to overtake ends. You see this happening in all of life, especially when money is involved. Mammon strives to be in control, to win a person's ultimate loyalty.

Here's the question we must ask: Do we have money, or does money have us? We know that Mammon has got us in its deadly grip when we define ourselves in terms of bank account or possessions, when we imagine that what we have is who we are. This is the delusion of fools. We are always different from our wealth. We can own shelves of great classics bound in the best Moroccan leather and still be illiterate; we can cover our walls with expensive art and have no love of beauty; we can own acres of land and be small-minded.

And I think God called him a fool for another reason: *he planned for the future but neglected eternity.* Oh, he was going to enjoy a great retirement, have a wonderful time traveling and dining in the best restaurants; they would maybe even put in that swimming pool they had been dreaming about. They would live it up! But then what? What would happen when the angel of death came and separated him from his things? There are no pockets in shrouds, as they say, no safe deposit boxes in coffins. He had planned for life's every contingency but neglected life's only inevitability.

If money is the measure of a person, as many think, it is so only because it can show how small we are. The limitations of money are dangerous, setting before us the temptation to become even more obsessed with material things and thus more under the influence of Mammon. But they can also help us learn that, in fact, we are something different from what we own, that our wealth cannot be measured by bank statements and can never be affected by the fate of our investments; they can assure us that neither bulls nor bears running down Wall Street have anything to do with who we are and what matters in life. These inevitable limitations—having more wants than money can satisfy—can remind us that we are not only bodies but souls, and they can reveal how large we really are.

13

Playing Monopoly without Getting into a Fight

The Limitations of Competitiveness

I've never understood people who don't play to win. The half-hearted leave me wholly mystified; the lukewarm leave me cold. If you want to be in the game, throw yourself into it—unreservedly. Put all your money on the table, and never say uncle, never give up, never go to the shower knowing you could have tried harder. Otherwise, why bother?

A few months ago my wife and I were lounging on Coronado Beach, reading novels and burrowing feet in the sand and listening to the rhythmic crash of waves, when I decided to go for a run. An hour later I returned, with cockiness pumping harder than my heart, and I said, "I've just whipped the Navy SEALS!"

This was true, mostly.

What happened was this. I had headed north along the meandering surf line, quickly losing myself in the beauty of a dark blue sea that with distant decisiveness turned into pale blue sky, the darting congregations of snowy plovers huddled against a vast beach, and the little sand-crusted engineers, with sagging swimsuits, building their fortresses and throwing seaweed at each other. But I didn't notice the SEALS running toward me until they were quite close. They were in formation, about twenty of them, with an officer barking orders at their side; their brown T-shirts and shorts were soaked with sweat. As we passed, one of them, with muscles that bolstered my confidence in our national security and with more adrenaline running through his system than he knew how to manage, turned to me when I was about four feet from him and screamed, "YEAH!"

I nearly had a heart attack. I jumped back, terrified I had somehow incited their wrath. I was about to salute or hum the Navy Hymn or maybe fall on my knees to beg for mercy when I realized he was being friendly. He was offering encouragement to an old guy with white hair who could still manage to run; he was making me a comrade in the struggle for fitness, a brother of the company of the muscle-hardened, an honorary SEAL. I waved and said "Hey!" back to him, relieved to be alive.

I continued north as they headed south, and by the time I turned around they were small specks, barely visible to me. But after awhile the specks appeared larger. It had to be my imagination, I told myself. If they were larger, I was gaining on them. Could this be? Could I be running faster than the SEALS? This possibility was too sweet. I pictured myself cruising by them, barely breathing, casually glancing at them with a patronizing smile that indicated they were doing pretty well, and then I might mention I had been running longer than they had been alive, that if they kept working at it, perhaps they, too, could someday be in fine shape. "Stay at it, boys," I would say as I flashed a thumbs-up, passing them with my final sprint.

Imagining this energized me. I picked up my pace, running faster than usual. I was taking them, sure enough; realizing this, I didn't just want to catch them but to beat them, to pound their skinny backsides into the sand. By the time I was about a hundred yards from them, the race had become an epic struggle—me against the United States Navy—and I was winning. This would serve the national interest, I told myself, by humiliating them into working harder; I wanted to do my part for our country. I was pushing hard, an efficient machine, a heart-and-lungs-and-muscle wonder, a cheetah chasing prey across the Serengeti Plain.

Then one of the SEALS stumbled and fell over. That was my first clue that they had probably been running farther than I. I tried not to notice him throwing up as I ran past, still determined to show them my stuff. As I came alongside their stumbling formation I slowed to their pace, and then, to be friendly, especially now that I was an honorary SEAL, I smiled and said, "How far you guys gone today?"

One turned his head toward me with a dazed, confused look, as if I had spoken Swahili, and then he turned to the others for help, my question the last, impossible challenge of the day. One groaned out, "About twenty miles, maybe twenty-five."

I suddenly saw myself: a slug crawling along in the slime of my arrogance. I wasn't worthy to brush sand off their stinking feet. In retrospect, I wish I had said, "Thanks for your hard work," and then stopped, out of respect, out of deference to them. But the competitive drive had not yet drained out of my system, so I said, "Thanks for your hard work," and then I turned up the burners and raced ahead.

Eventually I told my wife they had been running a marathon. And that they were wearing boots.

There may be some truth to what my family and friends say: I'm a competitive person.

The American Way

Well, judging from the way my family and friends fight back when they're smashing tennis balls or playing cards or arguing politics, I'm not alone! A single game of Monopoly can create enough relational wounds to keep Dr. Phil busy for a month.

Speaking of which, though we may not hope for a monopoly in real life, we would at least like an economic advantage, and this means we must learn how to compete in the marketplace. Our economy is based on competition, and so important is this to our national well-being, so fundamental to our national psyche, that we have created a culture that is probably more competitive than any before it (in competition over competition, we'd win!). In our most telling myths we extol the rugged individualist, the one who with red blood and large stones rides by himself into the frontier of his fortune, and, dadgummit, prevails against every adversary and over every obstacle until he makes a success of himself.

Playing to win is the American way. If you're a loser in this country, the best you can hope for is to be ignored; if you're a winner, though, you're set up on a pedestal and rewarded with admiration and affection. We love winners, so, out of parental concern, we teach our children to be competitive—in school, on the playground, in their first jobs. We do this not simply to help them succeed, but to shape their characters, to instill within them virtues of toughness and courage. We want them to know that even if you're on your own one-yard line with ten seconds left on the clock, and you're too tired to move a single muscle, you keep playing, you throw the Long Bomb—the Hail Mary—and you hope to high heaven your receiver gets there in time to catch it. That's the American way.

We *believe* in competition.

And if this isn't enough, there's another reason we try so hard: we *need* to come out on top. Our nagging sense of vulner-

132

ability in a dangerous world fuels our competitive fires. If we win—the game, the position, the argument, the election, the relationship—we'll *be* winners; we *ourselves* will be victorious, have worth, be somebody, maybe even hero enough to deny the approach of death for a moment or two. Our feelings of insecurity make us eager and willing students of our culture's central lesson.

Out of the Game

But the other limitations considered in this book lead inevitably to the end of competitiveness. When your body wears out, athletic competitiveness deteriorates; arthritic knees make it hard to run marathons, or even hold your own in a pick-up game at the YMCA. When your mind loses its sharp edge, winning the Nobel Prize becomes less likely. When your confidence slips into uncertainty, the will to win slackens, if not stops. All the limitations of life conspire to make it more difficult to compete, thus forcing you to face yet more limitations, the limitations of competitiveness.

It's tempting to argue that these only shift the direction of competitive instincts: now they turn inward. So if you're playing golf, you're no longer interested in beating others in your foursome but beating yourself, conquering some part of you that wreaks havoc with your swing. I use this illustration for a reason: golf is a game in which you regularly hear people say that you really only play against yourself. If that's true—and I doubt it—it might explain why golfers tend to be an unhappy lot: they can never win without beating some part of themselves. But I confess that I appreciate golfers the way runners appreciate bikers or sailors appreciate motorboaters; the thought of them challenges my Christian charity. I'm projecting my own frustration onto them, no doubt. It goes back to my last game—on the Old Course at St. Andrews, Scotland. My first drive, executed in front of a gallery of tourists from around the world, dribbled about fifty yards. When I walked out to my ball, a man was waiting for me in his golf cart. He pointed to the eighteenth green and in a thick Scottish brogue said, "You better go that way, lad." This did not build my confidence, and my game deteriorated rapidly. I decided that the country where golf began would be a good place to end it, which created a kind of poetic symmetry. I suppose golfers would say that competing against myself was too daunting.

But I digress. My point is that playing against yourself is not really competition, or, if so, only a pale form of the real thing, a sign that you're only good for a game where you ride around in an electric cart and pretend not to care whether you win or lose. Competition for most of us still means beating competitors, triumphing over adversaries. You can run along the beach for many miles, and it may be fine exercise and an opportunity to commune with nature, but it's not competition till you're burning your lungs to overtake Navy SEALS. This is what's threatened by the limitations of competitiveness. We may be able to do all sorts of things, but we can no longer stay in the game, no longer pit ourselves against others, no longer believe we'll become winners.

Pure Delight

Here's the consolation: when we cannot contend between the triumph of victory and the agony of defeat, we're free to enjoy the game itself. Put another way, when we no longer need to win, we can experience the deeper, purer pleasure of love.

Let me explain. I've come to believe that the opposite of love is not hate. If love is directed to the other—honoring and delighting and serving the other—hate is similarly oriented. Though hate is different—turning honor into dishonor, delight into disgust, and serving into hurting—it nonetheless remains directed to the other. The true opposite to love is pride: pride is wholly directed to the self; it is what theologians describe as the original sin, "the heart turned in on itself." The temptation for our first parents, as we've already seen in Genesis 3, was not to hate each other, but to eat fruit from "the tree of the knowledge of good and evil." If Adam and Eve did this, they were told, they would "be like God." *The* original human failure is to want to be more than human, to want to take God's place. What does it mean to be like God, if not to be at the center of things, in control, the Master of the Universe, or at least of the Master of My Little Universe?

This is not easy to pull off, of course, and the anxiety it creates must be assuaged, so we struggle for assurance that we're really worthy of the top. A winner! To a certain extent we might enjoy tennis, for example, but what we really enjoy is winning, defeating opponents, proving ourselves *better* than others. In this sense, we use the game and our competitors for selfish purposes. Our pride conscripts almost everything into the battle of defending our place at the center.

I once heard a man speak lovingly about his horse. The man's name, fittingly, was Morgan. His horse wasn't a blue ribbon champion, but he had deep affection for it. One day he met another horseman, someone who was quick to list all the superior characteristics of his own horse. Morgan said, "You know, it became clear to me that this man didn't love his horse as much as he loved having a better horse than I."

I've never forgotten that comment. When I owned the sailboat I mentioned in the last chapter, I moored it in Sausalito, a Marin County enclave of great wealth. At the marina were fabulous yachts—forty- and fifty-foot vessels of gleaming, sleek beauty. After a while I noticed that many of them never left the dock. I thought of Morgan's comment, and I wondered if the owners of those yachts loved having a better boat more than they loved the boat itself. I wondered if, on the rare occasions they might have taken their boats out, they loved having a faster boat more than sailing; I wondered if they loved bragging at the yacht club more than being close hauled in a twenty-knot wind. Pride's gravitational pull is so powerful it can pull anything, even sailboats, into its orbit.

I've had my own struggles with pride, to be sure, but not in the case of my sailboat. Pride took one look at my extremely modest twenty-year-old craft and immediately turned toward other, more promising venues for its mischief. Whatever pride I had in the *Jennifer Lee* was of a wholly innocent type, if indeed pride is even the right word. I simply delighted in that boat for its own sake; I loved her *as a boat,* and for no other reason.

Okay, once my chest swelled a bit—the first time I soloed in San Francisco Bay in a strong wind. For a moment I wondered how many sailors could have done it. Pride peeked over the sill of my consciousness, but I quickly beat it senseless by remembering some of my Major Screw-Ups on the Water, the times I ran aground, was nearly run over by tankers and ferries, almost sank in the middle of the bay and drowned my crew. That dropped me to my knees with a prayer of gratitude for the angels' protection.

I once took Bob out with me. He was a member of the faculty of the seminary I served, and I was glad to have him along for the ride, though I couldn't help noticing he enjoyed my hobby more than I enjoyed his. He had recently taken up the violin. His wife had insisted he practice in the back of the house, which unfortunately put him closer to my own house—a significant problem, because he practiced at three o'clock in the morning with open windows. My dedication to the fine arts in general and music in particular was sorely strained by the rough sawing of *Claire de Lune.* But for the first ten minutes of tossing in bed, I would smile, even chuckle to myself, happy to be reminded of someone who so loved making music that he would make a fool of himself in front of the neighborhood, not to mention the audience at recitals where he performed alongside eight-year-olds, someone who knew he would never be anything more than a mediocre player. There was something so pure in his newfound passion, so unself-conscious, that I suspect God kept smiling as I began to grumble because of my sleeplessness.

As a younger man, far more intent on saving the world, or at least saving my reputation in it, I didn't respect the time people spent on hobbies; in my highfalutin judgment, there were more important ways to invest one's energies. But in growing older I've grown younger, and now I have a higher regard for the manifold blessings of play. Few things are lovelier, if you ask me, than a woman with arthritic fingers starting organ lessons because she had always loved hearing Bob Ralston on the *Lawrence Welk Show*; or a man who cultivates orchids, not to win first prize at the county fair, but because whenever he tries to describe the beauty of a white *Phalaenopsis* he gets an embarrassing lump in his throat; or someone, like my friend Bill, who keeps playing tennis, even with macular degeneration destroying his eyesight, even though he knows he will never win another match, simply because he loves the game, always has and always will. These people love something, not because it makes them better than someone else, not because it's useful in securing their worth, not because it makes them winners, but simply *for itself*. If this isn't exactly the sort of love that will arrive with the kingdom of God, it can't be far from it. To be sure, it's more important to love people, but I would argue that to love an orchid for its own sake, to delight in its *otherness,* is a significant way down the road toward being able to love people, not for what they do for us but for who they are.

If the limitations of competitiveness can free us for this, then bring them on.

137

14

The World Didn't Even Notice
When I Quit Trying to Save It

The Limitations of Responsibility

To grow in maturity we must accept responsibility; to keep growing we must accept the limitations of responsibility.

When we were young, we had to learn the disciplines of responsibility. Our parents required us to clean our bedrooms, or at least to clear a path into them; they expected us to keep our promises to feed the goldfish and mow the lawn; they nagged us about homework and attended parent-teacher conferences to see whether it got done. When we became adolescents, they advised us to choose our friends carefully; they warned us about the dangers of alcohol and drugs; they required us to pay half our car insurance. They breathed a sigh of relief when we became young adults who won the confidence of employers. They rejoiced when we committed ourselves to marriage partners, and they became almost giddy with delight when we fussed and worried about our own children, no doubt seeing in this proof that we had become what they had hoped and prayed and sometimes doubted we would become—responsible adults.

But after years of learning how to be responsible, after having others depend on us, after being in the center of our worlds and feeling so . . . *necessary,* we find ourselves facing a new reality: there are limitations to our responsibility. No matter how willingly we assume the problems of this world, and no matter how effectively we might solve them, we discover there is only so much one person can do—and it's usually much less than we imagine.

To maintain the trajectory of growth, we have to let go of responsibility as completely as we had to accept it in the first place. This is not to say that we are to become irresponsible, in the sense of shirking legitimate duties. But given our own fallibility and finitude, as well as the freedom of others, we must acquiesce to the limitations of what we can do.

This is not easy for two reasons. First, being needed by others feels good; responsibility is not only a burden but a boost—a boost to our sense of personal worth. After all, we like being in God's place, as we've seen, situated in the center of a little universe of our own making. Disquieting doubts, however, sooner or later trouble every usurper to the throne, and this inner agitation finds an effective sedative in the dependence of others. If my wife needs my love, if my children trust my wisdom, if my friends rely on my influence, if my employer considers me indispensable, if my parents look to me the way I used to look to them—if I'm *needed* for the well-being of others—well, I must be important, somehow deserving of this place at the center of things!

The second reason it's hard to accept the limitations of responsibility is because those depending on us are often the ones we love most, the ones with whom we are bound through family or friendship. Our motivation goes well beyond an insecure ego; it also springs from the heart. Affection mobilizes all the forces at our command to provide help. If those we love are in deep trouble, we want to do everything possible to pull them up from the pit.

Not God

But our arms are too short to reach some people. There are some things we cannot fix, and, if we try, we make matters worse. To be sure, there are many problems we should seek to amend and many people to whom we should extend help, so far as we are able. But the key phrase is *so far as we are able.* The little secret we don't like to admit is that none of us is God, not when it really gets down to it and someone needs saving.

Even if you or I were God, we'd have to contend with one pesky problem: human freedom. What makes this a problem, of course, is that people have it and are under the impression that they have a right to exercise it. This creates difficulties, as the sorry history of our race amply proves. If I were God, I'd be inclined to do away with it; then again, if I *were* God, I'd transcend that temptation and protect it for reasons I'd have to be God to understand. God apparently values human freedom enough to withdraw sovereignty to make room for it. That leaves us with little choice but to do the same.

Frederick Buechner, in his memoir *Telling Secrets,* speaks of his daughter's anorexia nervosa and the anguish he felt as he watched her nearly starve herself to death.

> The only way I knew to be a father was to take care of her, as my father had been unable to take care of me, to move heaven and earth if necessary to make her well, and of course I couldn't do that. I didn't have either the wisdom or the power to make her well. None of us has the power to change other human beings like that, and it would be a terrible power if we did, the power to violate the humanity of others even for their own good. The psychiatrists we consulted told me I couldn't cure her. The

best thing I could do for her was to stop trying to do anything. I think in my heart I knew they were right, but it didn't stop the madness of my desperate meddling, it didn't stop the madness of my trying. Everything I could think to do or say only stiffened her resolve to be free from, among other things, me. Her not eating was a symbolic way of striking out for that freedom. The only way she would ever be well again was if and when she freely chose to be. The best I could do as her father was to stand back and give her that freedom even at the risk of her using it to choose for death instead of life.

The best we can do sometimes is to stand back, to respect the freedom of others. The wife of an alcoholic may have to resist the overwhelming temptation to make excuses for him and instead let him flounder and maybe even drown in the life he has chosen. The father of a drug-dealing son may have to stop lecturing him and stop providing him a place to live and stop bailing him out of jail and stop paying for an attorney. An employee may have to walk away from her work to attend to the needs of her family, even if the next day her boss will rant and rave and threaten to fire her for not finishing the project. A husband may have to resign from the impossible task of guaranteeing his wife's happiness, realizing that no human being can ever do that for another. A daughter may have to give up trying to make her parents understand why she has decided on a career that will likely leave her little opportunity for marriage and a family.

Sometimes it's no longer your responsibility, if it ever was.

After failure in my life that hurt others and myself, I did my best to apologize and ask forgiveness; I worked hard to explain my actions and demonstrate my sorrow; I tried to repair the situation and make things better for everyone. But I was like a man in quicksand: the more I flailed about in my attempts to be responsible, the deeper I sank. Eventually, too weary to do anything else, I set the burden down. I can't say that I had reasoned my way through to a clearer understanding of human

141

behavior or that I found a deeper faith in the grace of God, though there were days when this was certainly true. Mostly, to tell the truth, I just got too tired of hanging on to whatever it was that I was hanging on to. So I let go. And then I seemed to hear God say, "Well, finally! It's about time you relaxed, boy. You're only human." I could not change my past, I could not control the reactions of others, and I could not fix everything that had gone wrong. If the past had some painful parts to it, well, God would have to provide the healing. If others were still angry with me, they would have to stay angry or get over it. If some things were still broken, life would have to carry on in the midst of the broken fragments.

Freedom for Others

There is only so much any of us can do, and though it's not easy to accept this, there are some consolations that come our way when we do.

The first is the joy of giving. When we honor the limitations of responsibility, we grant others a precious freedom—the freedom to live their own lives, for better or worse. That includes the freedom to find their own way out of some difficulties, which may be the only way toward authentic healing and growth. In accepting the limitations of our humanity, we often make room for others to develop the potential of their own. People need to be able to select their own rowboats and pull their own oars. If a boat starts taking on water, the one who's rowing should decide whether to fix it or tread water or swim for the shore. If we, by an inflated sense of responsibility, do not allow this, those under our care will either remain passively dependent or become aggressively independent to break out of the sphere of our influence. Few things are more pathetic than an individual who, out of excessive dependency, is paralyzed by a desperate need for approval. Unless perhaps it is an individual who, out of excessive independence, relentlessly and even ruthlessly ignores others in the pursuit of selfish desires. To help others avoid these extremes and become both strong and sensitive, both assertive and considerate, we must at times draw back to let them succeed or fail on their, and then, in either case, stay connected to them with truth-telling and understanding and faithful support.

Still vivid in my memory are the first steps that my children took. To see them actually stand on their own and then discover that they could put one foot in front of the other and so propel themselves across the room was, I suppose, more exciting for me than for them—until they got near the coffee table! Of course I rushed to grab them, protecting them from falling and hitting their heads on the edge. But there came a day, not many weeks later, when I had to let them keep walking not only near coffee tables but on hard sidewalks and steep stairways, and it *seemed* like not many weeks later that I had to watch them drive off in the car by themselves. Every part of my body tensed with worry when my daughters got near danger, and it took all the self-restraint I could summon not to rescue them from all risks. But if I deserve any credit for parenting, it's not only for doing things right but also for sometimes having the sense *not* to do things that also felt very right. To allow others to mature, we have to let them discover and nurture their own sense of responsibility, and that means surrendering our own.

Freedom for Ourselves

As difficult as this may be, it is also an immense relief. To feel responsible for everything, you either have to be God or expect to go nuts. If you think you're God, please put this book down and immediately find a psychiatrist. But if you know you're not God and still want to be responsible for everything, please consider how utterly impossible and downright stupid this is, or you also will need a psychiatrist. No one except God can carry the weight of everyone's safety and health and happiness and fulfillment in life. To guarantee this for even one person will soon have anxiety tearing you apart like a lion enjoying a fine meal.

As vivid in my memory as my children's first steps—more vivid, actually—is the acute worry I sometimes felt about the bad things that could happen to them. One day I was in my recliner, letting my mind wander down the road of possible disasters that could overtake them, and an acidic, burning fear rose from the depths of my being. I was responsible for them! The burden of this was heavier than planet Earth, something I knew I couldn't bear. In what I now believe was a moment of divine grace, a miracle of God's mercy, I suddenly saw that I could not be their father, not the father they needed, not a father with power to guide and protect them. They needed a much better father than I. They needed nothing less than a Heavenly Father.

A great relief swept over me when I realized that was exactly what they had. I could be their human father, and I would do my best in that role, but I could not be God for them. So in the days and years to come, I would often form a mental picture of lifting them up into the presence of God, and I would say, "Here, Lord, take them and care for them. I trust you to lead them with perfect wisdom and to surround them with abundant love." Though I sometimes still worried, and though I sometimes lifted them up to God but forgot to let go, for the most part the intolerable burden was lifted. I became free to be nothing more and nothing less than I really was: their earthly father, filled with love but possessing only limited responsibility.

As we have already seen, to be content with our limited humanity liberates us from striving for the impossible, making possible a greater peace and joy. The limitations of responsibility may not be easy; accepting them may cut against the grain of our personalities. But they remind us that we're only human, and this confers a great consolation.

15

When Someone Else Needs to Drive

The Limitations of Control

Every other week I visit a friend who lives in a convalescent home. The facilities are well maintained, bright and cheery; the nursing staff is excellent, friendly and competent; and my friend is a delight, regaling me with stories and bolstering me with encouragement. All the same, I have a vague discomfort. I think I know what causes it: a fear of losing control. Examples of how this could happen abound in a convalescent home. Some residents are unable to leave the premises without assistance from relatives or friends; some are confined to wheelchairs; some need others to translate incoherent mutterings; some have lost command of bladder and bowels. I don't like being reminded of the possibility of these things.

Few things frighten us more than losing control. Each loss, no matter how apparently minor, is a blow to our freedom, a blow to our ability to assert ourselves, a blow to our humanity.

My mother-in-law approached her eightieth birthday with dread, knowing she would not be able to renew her driver's license because of deteriorating eyesight. Sure enough, when the day came, she had to surrender her right to drive. I assumed she would sell her car. Why keep it sitting in the garage? Why pay insurance and automobile club fees for something she couldn't use? But for her a different logic was at work. The car was a symbol of freedom that she didn't want to relinquish. Moreover, an empty garage would be a symbol, too, and one she didn't want to acknowledge. So she kept the old Chevy for over a year, doing nothing with it except occasionally starting it to keep the battery and maybe something inside her from dying. When finally she consented to sell it, it was a very sad day.

She recently said to me, "It's *so* hard not being able to drive. I'm dependent on others to go shopping, to get my hair done, to go to the bank. I don't like not having my freedom."

The Pleasure of Surrender

Without denying the difficulty of needing someone else to drive, I want to suggest that having someone else behind the wheel offers a consolation. I say this with caution, even reticence. I presently enjoy so much personal mobility that for me to speak about the blessings of losing control of one's life may seem insensitive, even callous. But truth is complex and multisided; a more complete view of reality often demands that we see several different, competing sides of an issue at the same time. Yes, it can be painful to lose one's freedom, to be robbed of self-assertion and self-governance. Nonetheless, this, too, is true: this loss grants a fine pleasure—the pleasure of surrender.

To illustrate this, I want to refer again to an experience I had while sailing on San Francisco Bay. The wind suddenly shifted, catching the backside of my sail. As the boom swung across the stern, I reached up to slow it down. This was not smart. I learned the hard way what a flying boom can do to a stationary arm: the arm doesn't remain stationary for long. When mine moved, it did so without using any of my existing joints, which had the unfortunate consequence of creating a brand new joint in the middle of my upper arm.

At first I wasn't aware of pain. I only knew my arm didn't go where I told it to go. This was weird, almost as weird as seeing it dangling at my side at an exceedingly odd angle to the rest of my body. When things started to spin around me I decided it was time to sit down and issue orders for our return to Sausalito.

The only one present was my mother. She was an eager crew member, doing her best to work the lines and trim the sail and move the tiller, but her eyes, darting from son to sail to water, had a terror that brought me to my senses. I couldn't rely on her to sail back to the marina. What if I passed out? Then we'd *really* be in trouble. So I asked her to get on the radio and call for help.

Within minutes another sailboat, with two men on board, came alongside us. One of them jumped into our boat to take control. He knew what he was doing. He started the engine, told us everything would be all right, and piloted us through the choppy waters toward home. He was a retired Navy chaplain, he said, and his friend in the boat behind us was a doctor. I felt a great relief. I no longer had to be in control, which meant I no longer needed to worry. I could surrender. I could relax in the arms of a competent providence that was going to handle the crisis.

I breathed a prayer of gratitude for God's protection. I did think it might have been slightly better if the chaplain had stayed in the boat behind us and the doctor had jumped into our boat, but I decided that was quibbling with the Almighty.

When we tied up at the marina, the doctor examined my arm. He said he was afraid that if they tried to move me I might fall in the water, and then we'd have another serious problem. Did

I mind if he called the paramedics? I assured him I was more than willing to wait, especially if it meant staying out of the water. When the paramedics arrived, they swarmed around me with concern and efficiency and strength, and what I remember most about those moments was the deep calm I had, the almost perfect peace that came from my surrender to their care. Even as the ambulance seemed to aim for every bump in the road, causing pain to shoot through my body with every bounce, I felt myself relax in an astonishing way. Someone caring was at my side, and someone who knew the way was at the wheel. Surrendering to these paramedics did not remove the pain, of course, but it was an undeniable pleasure—a pleasure I would have rather done without, to be sure, but one I was happy to receive as a consolation.

Can you recall something similar in your life? Perhaps it was the secret delight you felt when, as a child, you woke up with enough of a cold to stay home from school, and you knew you could lie in bed while your mother fussed over you all day long. Perhaps it was the surprising relief of boot camp, where your personal identity was stripped from you and you were told what to do and where to go and what to think. Perhaps it was the ecstasy of falling in love and happily submitting not only to the embrace but also to the desires of another.

What was it about these situations that felt so good? At one level, they might have been painful, something you wouldn't have chosen for yourself; they might have been unhealthy for your psychological and spiritual growth. At another level, though, they offered a secret satisfaction, a compensating comfort. Why?

The answer lies in our nature. We are human, and this means we exist in the difficult tension between self-surrender and self-assertion. We are relational beings who need to be part of something larger than ourselves, part of an all-encompassing whole; yet, we are also personal beings who need to develop our own unique identities. This puts us in an impossible bind.

We can describe this from the standpoint of psychology. We begin life in our mother's arms. As infants, we make no distinction between ourselves and this warm and nurturing and protecting embrace. But as our sense of self develops, as we come to perceive an *I* over against a *Thou*, we gradually assert our own wills and begin the quest for our own self-expression. Psychologists speak of this process as individuation, the process of separating ourselves from our parents to find our true selves. This is never easy, so comforting is our mother's embrace and so terrifying is our consequent vulnerability. But what else can we do? To become fully human, we must assert ourselves; to mature, we must leave our mother's arms and seek our own uniqueness. The more successful we are, however, the more alienated and homesick we become, and the more we want to belong to an all-powerful and all-encompassing whole.

Or we can describe this in theological terms. The biblical story of creation says we were made in God's image, and, as part of that gift, we were given the task of subduing the earth. But when, in an expression of that freedom, we chose to eat the forbidden fruit that would open our eyes and make us "like God," when, instead of being content with submitting to the God in whose image we had been made, we grasped at something more, reached for independence, for god-like autonomy to be and do as we pleased, we got our wish: we were allowed to stray. We are now vulnerable to death, alienated from the source of our life. Built into the structure of our humanity, in other words, is the desire both to journey to the far country and to return home; we want both to be free and to be united with the ground of our being.

That is why we feel a certain relief, even pleasure, when circumstances beyond our choosing strip self-control out of our hands and force us to surrender. Each little submission revives the nearly forgotten memory of our mother's embrace and, before that, our Father's.

Dependent on a Powerful Force

We want to be independent, assertive, in control of ourselves and subduing the world around us. We also want to be united with something larger than ourselves, submissive, dependent on a powerful force.

This may help explain why some people willingly submit to destructive relationships. A woman, for example, may stay married to a domineering man who crushes her spirit and even abuses her, while her family and friends watch with uncomprehending dismay. Why won't she pack her baggage and hit the road before he unloads more of his baggage and hits her body? Different psychological dynamics may be at work, but, among them, this is likely: she "enjoys"—if only at an unconscious level—her loss of control, her surrender to a higher power.

Or consider the case of otherwise rational people who become part of a cult that requires them to sell their possessions and submit to the outrageous demands of a "spiritual leader." What would motivate them to abdicate so fully their minds and wills? One reason, surely, is the satisfaction that comes with complete surrender.

I was recently asked to write an article about people who believe they've been abducted by extraterrestrial aliens. This is not a subject I would have come up with on my own; I'm not a fan of *Star Trek*, and I never read science fiction. But precisely because of my naiveté, I thought it might be interesting to investigate the matter. To my surprise, little searching was required to find people willing to talk about their "abductions." I heard from seemingly ordinary people dramatic testimonials to space ships, bodily probing, stolen ova, manipulated time, and all manner of space creatures. One common theme was

150

that of surrendering to an overpowering force. They were taken by flying saucers up into giant mother ships, wherein various biological experiments were conducted on them. The abductees, through all their ordeals, never resisted, never fought back. Not only did they willingly yield to a superior force, they seemed to find it peaceful, almost pleasurable. One woman told of being carried off by robot-like creatures who lifted her into a "rose-colored light," and as she ascended from the earth, "the rose turned into many beautiful colors." The woman's name, not incidentally, was Rose. She surrendered to a force that enabled her to rise above and become more than herself.

Herein lies the appeal of all space aliens, domineering lovers, harsh bosses, arrogant commanders, corrupt politicians, religious fanatics, and egomaniacal dictators: a part of us is weary with trying to be in control and finds more than a little relief in submission; a part of us wants to submit to a power than can lift us into a rainbow of colors.

Divine Madness

Now, if the above is true, an important question must be asked: submission to whom, or to what? This makes all the difference. It's possible to submit to forces that ultimately harm us; we can, and often do, cede control to people or ideologies or institutions that keep us dependent and thwart our growth. But it's also possible to relinquish ourselves to benevolent powers, from whose nurturing breasts we draw strength to grow into our own individuality.

Marriage illustrates both these possibilities. If you surrender to a selfish, domineering spouse who, out of insecurity or some other neurosis, squishes you under a thumb of authority, your own humanity will be undermined and diminished. But if you surrender to a loving, encouraging spouse who, out of security or some other healthy trait, lifts you on the arms of support, your own humanity will be expanded and enhanced.

Selfishness and ignorance, as with all human relationships, flaw even the best marriages, and thus every surrender entails unanswered loss. But what if it were possible to yield to a power so benevolent, so perfectly loving and lovingly perfect, that every loss became a greater gain, every throwing down of arms became a new empowerment, every meek obedience a strong assertion, every self-sacrifice a self-possession? The paradox would defy all earthly logic, and thus to imagine such a possibility, let alone hope for it, would require either madness or faith.

There is a madness in faith, too, but it's a divine madness, the Creator's folly that invites us to surrender ourselves fully in order to win ourselves wholly, that calls us to lose ourselves in eternal love only to find ourselves in uniqueness. This, according to the New Testament, was the experience of Jesus Christ, who "emptied himself . . . and became obedient to the point of death—even death on a cross. Therefore God also highly exalted him and gave him the name that is above every name."

A Reminder

Every loss of control, it seems to me, brings with it this consolation: it tells us who we are. The pleasure we feel in surrender, however secret and small, reminds us of the bind in which we exist, the dual desire to be part of a larger whole and yet individually separate, to lose ourselves and yet gain ourselves. It reminds us, further, that the final resolution of this tension is found only in God.

You might think a reminder like this is scant compensation for the suffering that accompanies some losses. The above thoughts may seem only a pedantic and ultimately futile attempt to find good in plainly bad circumstances.

I can only say that apparently weak and insignificant things can be transformed by faith into strong and significant things. The ordinary can become extraordinary. For Christians, a sprinkling of tap water becomes baptism into the Living Water; a piece of bread and a sip of wine become communion with Christ. And every loss of control and the surrender it demands can be a kind of sacrament, a small participation in the surrender to God who more than compensates for every loss.

16

Are We Still Having Fun?
The Limitations of Pleasure

Life is full of many pleasures. There are physical pleasures: the smells of bacon frying, a baby after a bath, and a bouquet of roses; the tastes of coffee in the morning, wine in the evening, and creme brulee for dessert; the touches of a warm shower, silk pajamas, and your beloved's caress; the sounds of a Mozart concerto, your children laughing, and the wind in aspens; the sights of mist on a quiet lake, the iridescence of a hummingbird, and a smile on your spouse's face after a fight.

There are other delights too: the relational pleasures of loyal friendship and undeserved forgiveness; the intellectual pleasures of perceiving a new truth and grasping a complicated argument; the moral pleasures of protecting life and serving justice; the spiritual pleasures of sensing God's favor and expressing heartfelt praise.

When these pleasures combine, the ecstasy can be nearly explosive. Think of sex: as physical sensations join forces

154

with relational and even spiritual pleasures . . . well, how many poems have been written attempting to describe this without ever quite succeeding?

Pleasures, though, come to an end. No matter how good something may be in itself, our delight in it inevitably will fade. Paradoxically, we hunger for a satiation that ultimately destroys our appetite. Passionate lovemaking may transport you farther than your wildest fantasies, but eventually you're ready to read a book or make the coffee. And the limitations of pleasure are not limited to bodily ones; truth to tell, we also reach satiation with even moral and spiritual ones. The praise of God may be an endless joy for those in a state of perfection, but, this side of heaven, an hour or two of worship makes us more than ready to head to the fellowship hall for a potluck dinner. The thing itself—praise of God, for instance—does not diminish in its goodness, but our *experience* of pleasure in it wobbles, stumbles, and falls over exhausted. William Cowper said that "pleasure is labour too, and tires as much."

More Complex Pleasures

Before considering the consolations attending these limitations, let's begin by inquiring into their cause. Why do pleasures always end for us?

In his book *Orthodoxy,* G. K. Chesterton suggested an intriguing answer. Our problem, he said, is lack of vitality, a want of life. We are too easily bored.

A child kicks his legs rhythmically through excess, not absence of life. Because children have abounding vitality, because they are in spirit fierce and free, therefore they want things repeated and unchanged. They always say, "Do it again"; and the grown-up person does it again until he is nearly dead. For grown-up people are not strong enough to exult in monotony. But perhaps

155

God is strong enough to exult in monotony. It is possible that God says every morning, "Do it again" to the sun; and every evening, "Do it again" to the moon. It may not be automatic necessity that makes all daisies alike; it may be that God makes every daisy separately, but has never got tired of making them. It may be that He has the eternal appetite of infancy; for we have sinned and grown old, and our Father is younger than we. The repetition in Nature may not be a mere recurrence; it may be a theatrical *encore*.

Chesterton had a way of turning things upside down and making you believe he had set them right side up. Why should we think an impersonal, objective law says all grass must be green? Why not, rather, imagine a God who has not yet tired of green grass? Perhaps God possesses a limitless capacity for pleasure, a boundless joy that admits no boredom. And perhaps we, in wandering from God, have lost the holy and childlike capacity for tireless wonder. After all, didn't Jesus say that we must become as children to enter the kingdom of God?

There is wisdom in Chesterton's point, but it's a wisdom that disappears if we arrive at it too soon. My grandson has an almost inexhaustible delight in stories, but I hope one day he tires of hearing them read to him, so he learns how to read them himself. I hope he wearies of kitties and moves on to Aslan and eventually on to the Lion of Judah. My step-granddaughter loves to hear "Old MacDonald Had a Farm," and before I have finished singing it she says, "Again!" This is cute, for the time being. But I hope one day she gets bored with the ditty and moves on to U2 and finally gets bored with that, too, until she, please God, discovers J. S. Bach. It's one thing to remain childish; it's something else to grow through adulthood into becoming childlike. There is wisdom in simplicity, but only after one has suffered through complexity. If my grandson should become a theologian, he may return to *The Chronicles of Narnia* and be more deeply moved by these stories than when he was a child. His pleasure in Aslan will be deeper precisely because he was not content to remain with Aslan but cultivated other, more complex pleasures. If my step-granddaughter should become a symphony conductor, she may well return to American folk tunes and hear more in them than I ever have, but only because at one time she wanted something more and her pleasure-seeking restlessness moved her into rock and jazz and classical music.

Because we grow beyond some pleasures, they no longer satisfy. But I think the reverse may also be true: because some pleasures no longer satisfy, we grow beyond them. The limitations of pleasure—this is their first great consolation—keep us searching for new pleasure, and this restlessness leads us into experiences that help us grow into a larger humanity. Because the adventures of the Hardy Boys no longer satisfy, we might find ourselves aboard ship with Horatio Hornblower. When we've had enough of the sea, we might, in time, discover the pleasures of Kierkegaard. When we have had our fill of philosophy, we might, out of restlessness, plunge into the vastly more complex pleasures of loving another person. On and on it goes, the limitations of one pleasure leading us to another, and what *can* happen is this: as our experiences multiply—physical, relational, intellectual, moral, spiritual—our capacity for pleasure broadens and deepens. The pursuit of pleasure, especially if it follows the route of self-discipline and education, can lead to the enjoyment of increasingly complex pleasures, and these, in turn, can help us become more complex human beings.

I've always enjoyed the taste of grape juice. But one day, out of boredom or rebellion or a quest for sophistication, I tried wine. I *tried* it but didn't get down more than a few swallows before pouring the bottle into the sink. It was so bitter, why would poets write odes to it and lovers find stimulation in it and Jesus enjoin the drinking of it in remembrance of him? It was easier to stick with grape juice. But for some reason I tried another glass and then another, and at some point (maybe when

157

I poured from a bottle that cost more than $1.99) I began to notice something more than bitterness; I started to taste layers of activity in it—the fruit and acid, the bouquet of smells and flavors, all the sensations that would one day make grape juice seem utterly dull.

Drinking wine hasn't necessarily made me a better person, though there have been times when it provided a timely adjustment to my attitude. But it has certainly broadened my tastes and thus, in a small measure, has expanded me as a person. I have repeated this pattern many times, following pleasures into boredom and thus into newer, more complex pleasures, and it has been a central stimulus to my personal growth.

Without limitations in the pleasures of grape juice, we might never try wine; without limitations in the pleasures of wine, we might never pick up a book; without limitations in the pleasures of reading, we might never make time to make love; without limitations in the pleasures of sex, we might never get out of bed to get on with the rest of our lives. Spent pleasures can, over time, recover potency. The cause of yesterday's boredom can tomorrow rise with fresh delight. But my point is that, in general, the end of one pleasure can be a benevolent goad into other experiences that in turn enhance our lives.

A Child Again

However—and this is a mighty significant *however*—this restlessness, like all goads, is a sharp jab in the backside of our being. It hurts. As pleasures diminish we grasp for more, and after those pleasures diminish we grasp again, and on and on this goes, the grasping never ending. This creates an anti-pleasure, a gnawing pain in our hearts. As we jump from one thing to the next, we have an increasing sense that nothing will satisfy, *nothing*. This becomes a terrifying thought we try to suppress lest it overwhelm us with meaninglessness, even

158

despair. Why reach for one more pleasure? Why reach out to anything in life? Why not surrender to depression?

So if the limitations of pleasure can be a stimulus to new pleasures, and thus to growth, they can also become a source of suffering. To escape this suffering we might be tempted to grasp at new pleasures with greater intensity; to flee from emptiness, we might run faster and faster, becoming not broader and deeper but shallower. Even a cursory look at our national life proves that many, in fact, attempt to deal with the limitations of pleasure in this way. Our economy depends on all of us grasping after new things we really don't need; our culture jumps from one distraction to the next, like bugs skipping across the surface of water; our attention, even to serious subjects, spans no more than the time it takes to reach the next commercial break, which will be yet another encouragement to reach for one more thing that will not satisfy.

We encounter not just limitations in pleasure, then, but limitations in the *seeking* of pleasure. With this comes another potential consolation: out of weariness with the search for pleasure, out of a gathering conviction that nothing can satisfy our deepest hunger, we might—this is not automatic, but it can happen—reach one more time with a kind of final, desperate grasp at a pleasure that transcends all earthly pleasure, and we might take hold of nothing less than God. After falling exhausted, we might finally see something that has been there all along: a choice we must make between despair and faith.

If we choose the latter, thus opening ourselves to God, something wonderful is likely to happen: the Spirit of God will enter us and a transformation will begin. It will not be instantaneous; it will be so slow as to cause doubt about whether anything is really happening. But gradually our perspective will change; we will begin to see the world through the eyes of the Spirit. If God is love, a flicker of love will begin to burn within us; if God is just, a passion for justice will get aroused in our depths;

159

if God is forgiving, at least a desire to forgive others will start nudging its way into our hearts. St. Paul described "the fruits of the Spirit," the virtues that grow in us through the animating force of God, as "love, joy, peace, patience, kindness, generosity, faithfulness, gentleness, and self-control." And though the apostle didn't mention it, I doubt he would argue with an addition to the list: childlike simplicity. If Jesus said we must become as little children before entering the kingdom of God, then surely one of the first blessings of God's Spirit is the opportunity to become children again. Then perhaps we can partake of what Chesterton described as God's "eternal appetite of infancy."

We are now back to we where started. As T. S. Eliot said, "In my end is my beginning." The limitations of pleasure lead us toward newer pleasures and so help mature us into beings of greater complexity, and the inevitable dissatisfaction with this restless search for new pleasures can lead us to open ourselves to One who holds both simplicity and complexity in a unified whole, One who can take us by the hand and lead us back to the abounding vitality of childhood, back to the playground of this world, back to a spirit fierce and free that is strong enough, as Chesterton put it, to "exalt in monotony."

Now we have an endless fascination with things because our journey through complexity has enabled us to see them again for the first time. We come back to pleasures we had once experienced and long ago left, and now they resonate within us as never before. We have grown up enough to be children again, we have matured into an ability to appreciate simplicity.

A few weeks ago I was running along a country road not far from our home. The retiring sun was spreading a golden glow on the world, and my heart and lungs and muscles were working together like parts of a fine watch, and my mind and spirit were ambling along in peaceful aimlessness. Then suddenly I stopped. I had turned a corner and come upon something that rendered me motionless and robbed my breath more thoroughly than the previous five miles.

What I saw was a bougainvillea bush. I had run by it many, many times; through the years I had seen thousands of bushes just like it. That afternoon, though, I saw a bougainvillea bush again for the first time. The color of the flowers was a magenta so bold it seemed shameless. Each petal called attention to itself with flagrant immodesty, each seduced my eyes with what I can only describe as a kind of eternal purposefulness. I was transfixed. I don't know how long I stood there; it could have been a few seconds or a few hours, for I was in a dimension where time held no authority. And a feeling rose within me, eventually becoming a thought that erupted with considerable power. I knew that if I had never experienced anything before in my past and if I never experienced anything more in my future, this one sight would make life worthwhile, more valu-able than I could ever express in words. I had seen flowers like these before, no doubt many more beautiful, and I had taken pleasure in them and then gone on to other things, and I had no regret for doing so, but now, precisely after all the experi-ences of fifty-three years, precisely because those experiences in some way prepared me for this one, I was able to receive the simple gift of a bougainvillea bush in the afternoon and know I could never fully grasp it, never exhaust its meaning, never completely see its beauty.

The limitations of pleasure serve the blessed purpose in pushing us toward newer pleasures, and the limitations in this search serve an even more blessed purpose in bringing us back to the original pleasures and helping us see them again for the first time.

17

What Did You Say?

The Limitations of the Senses

What a wonder are our senses! Through them we apprehend the world around us and experience much of its pleasures and miseries.

The sense of smell, for instance, attracts and repels, elates and depresses, warns and calms. In an instant, aromas can alter your mood dramatically, eliciting intense delight or visceral disgust. Imagine a warm southern California evening. You're dining outdoors on the deck of a fine restaurant. The air is redolent with sea and eucalyptus and night-blooming jasmine and vanilla ice cream melting over warm cake and fresh coffee; your nose thinks it has ascended to heaven. Then someone at the table next to yours fires up a cigarette and smoke blows into your face, and then this same person has a gastric problem, which he attempts to solve—may God have mercy on his soul—with a secret, ever-so-slight emission that in the end (so to speak) has the subtlety of a stampeding herd of buffalo; your nose thinks it has descended to Hades. Then a young waiter walks by wearing Canoe cologne, and instantly you're transported back thirty-five years and you're sitting with your boyfriend in his '62 Chevy at Lookout Point. As Diane Ackerman put it, "Smells detonate softly in our memory like poignant land mines, hidden under the weedy mass of many years and experiences. Hit a tripwire of smell, and memories explode all at once. A complex vision leaps out of the undergrowth."

And taste! On an adult's tongue there are about ten thousand taste buds, each with about fifty cells that relay information through neurons to the brain. (Rabbits have seventeen thousand and cows have twenty thousand, which makes you wonder what we're missing; perhaps that's why they're still not bored with grass. Imagine how they'd react to pasta primavera.) Our taste buds are grouped together according to assignment, detecting salt, sour, sweet, or bitter—the manifold combination of which, along with food's aromas, make eating one of life's great pleasures. One bite of an orange makes you pity angels (who, presumably, have no need of physical sustenance). You might even wonder how heaven could really be heavenly if, with perfected bodies, we have no reason to eat, until you remember that the place itself was described by Jesus as a banquet table. It's not an exaggeration to say that a great meal, shared within a community of love, is a foretaste of heaven, a kind of appetizer before the main feast. So as you sit there in that restaurant, your taste buds are performing at least minor spiritual service for you. They bless you abundantly: first comes a basket of sourdough bread; then an appetizer of chilled jumbo shrimp arranged around cocktail sauce; then a bowl of lobster bisque; then the main course of salmon smothered with mango salsa, rice pilaf, and steamed vegetables; then "Death by Chocolate" and a French roast coffee. And throughout the whole meal, of course, "wine to gladden the human heart" (Psalm 104:14). You're having salmon? How about an Oregon pinot noir? Or perhaps a Sonoma Valley chardonnay? Each sip will rouse the taste buds to feverish activity, forging strange new alliances that can only be described by referring to other tastes, such as "hints of peach and apple, with a buttery base and an aftertaste of vanilla." But what if the chef had had a fight with his wife before work? What if he had been too preoccupied with her many faults to notice that the shrimp had turned bad? What if he had burned the salmon and overcooked the vegetables? And what if the wine had corked, turning vinegary and rancid? Well, it would be hard to work up the enthusiasm to give much of a tip!

And touch! The skin is our largest organ, the boundary between our bodies and the rest of creation. It can distinguish between the sting of nettles and the caress of a loved one—and with an intensity that momentarily empties the mind of every other thought and feeling. We could say that what we touch, or what touches us, goes through the skin to the brain and then to the heart; this sense, like the others, works on our emotions, arousing pleasure or inciting misery. So as you sit at the restaurant, you detect a breeze blowing across the water and the warmth of the outdoor heater; your fingers delight in the texture of the bread's crust and the silkiness of the silverware and the fine balance of stemware. Your lover reaches over to stroke your hand, while under the table he rubs his calf on yours, and just before the coffee is served he provides another dessert as he leans over to kiss you. You're not thinking about skin at a time like this, but if you were, you'd be mighty grateful for it, considering it one of your best friends. But the skin can not only turn you on but also turn on you. A squall hits the beach, and air like ice slices the back of your neck; the poison oak you accidentally brushed against that afternoon does its best to make you loathe your left ankle; and the waiter, walking by you, trips and drops a pitcher of ice water in your lap.

And hearing! The sound around us, sometimes melodious and sometimes cacophonous, binds us to life in this world; without sound we would be isolated, perhaps more alone than if we had lost any of our other senses. What we call sound is really

> an onrushing, cresting, and withdrawing wave of air molecules that begins with the movement of any object, however large or small, and ripples out in all directions. First something has to move—a tractor, a cricket's wings—that shakes the air molecules all around it, then the molecules next to them begin trembling, too, and so on. Waves of sound roll like tides to our ears, where they make the eardrum vibrate; this in turn moves three colorfully named bones (the hammer, the anvil, and the stirrup), the tiniest bones in the body. . . . The three bones press fluid in the inner ear against membranes, which brush tiny hairs that trigger nearby nerve cells, which telegraph messages to the brain: We *hear*.

What we hear can inform, inspire, inflame, incite. It can lead to understanding, lift to ecstasy, and throw into despair. Think of what music does to you, how it *transforms* you: the nerve mellowing of jazz or the pulse quickening of rock, the tear jerking of country or the soul ordering of baroque or the pathos evoking of opera. I wouldn't know how to describe what rap does to you, but it's still music, and even the worst of it does something preferable to what a jackhammer does outside your hotel window at 6:00 A.M. Your ears distinguish between these sounds. So as you sit at the restaurant, they happily receive the pounding of waves on sand, the slapping of water against moored boats, the occasional screech of gulls, the laughter of diners around you, the Mozart sonata coming from the little speakers under the eaves, and the clinking of your glasses as you and your dinner partner toast one another. When he leans over and says, "I love you," your ears devour the disturbance in the air waves, voraciously catching every nuance, every emphasis, every inflection. But the mood would change if, on the sand next to the restaurant patio, a kid turned up the volume on his boom box, forcing Eminem's crudities on you, or if next to you waiters put several tables together to accommodate about twenty people for an office party—a party that had already started in the lounge and was fast getting out of hand.

And sight! My heart breaks for those without this sense. I have often shut my eyes, as have all of us I suppose, and tried to imagine being born blind. I can't do it. *Imag*ination depends on images. With no images to draw upon, how can you conceive the world? "The greatest thing a human soul ever does in this world is to see something," said John Ruskin. "To see clearly is poetry, prophecy, and religion, all in one." Do we not cherish our eyes above other parts of the body, save those, like the heart, that are absolutely essential for life? Vision enables colors and textures and shapes and forms to register on our brains; it allows us to observe the downy fuzz on our baby's arms, or take in a panoramic sweep of the Grand Canyon. So as you sit at the restaurant, you see the sun silently sliding below the waterline, casting across the water toward you a golden highway of sparkling light; you see the white blossoms of the jasmine you had already smelled; you see words on the menu in your hands; and you see the other who is seeing you, the eyes of the man you love, and as you see *into* his eyes, you somehow know you're seeing into him. But as with the other senses, sight allows ugliness into our lives. You see the couple at a table near you fighting, so angry they won't look at each other; you see that your waiter has had an allergic reaction to something, the evidence of which is crusting the rims of his nostrils; on the way home from the restaurant, you see an accident, and the following evening you see on the news pictures of it that you will have a hard time forgetting.

The good and the bad, the beautiful and the ugly—our five senses take in all of life, allow us to receive and, in a way appropriate to our species, comprehend the world.

Steps toward Death

Diminishment of these senses is a serious matter, and diminish they do. If accident or disease don't harm them first, aging surely will. As we grow older we need spectacles, maybe even magnifying glasses. We annoy spouses by continually saying, "What?" We use larger amounts of salt and pepper and other spices to give food taste. We're unaware of smells, sometimes our own, that normally would have bothered us. We can't feel as much with leathery skin.

Most of these losses cause only minor inconvenience. I don't like needing reading glasses, because even though I have purchased nearly a truckload of the ten-dollar variety, stationing them on desks, by reading chairs, in bathrooms, in cars, and in pockets, I still can't find a pair when I need them. What happens to them is one of life's great mysteries. Lately, I've even considered getting a necklace that enables you to hang glasses around your neck, but that brings to mind too many matronly, bosomy teachers, and it seems just too much an admission of my advancing age. So I keep fuming about lost glasses and accusing my wife of stealing them—which sometimes she does, because she can't find hers.

Sometimes, though, the losses of our senses are more serious. My mother-in-law has had to contend not only with presbyopia but, worse, macular degeneration. With no close-up vision, she must rely on someone else to read the labels on her medicine bottles and pay her bills and tell her the price of items when she's shopping; she finds it difficult to watch TV, unless she's sitting only a few feet from the set. Her prognosis is discouraging: doctors say she will continue to lose her sight.

167

Of course the loss of one sense can increase the effectiveness of others. The blind and deaf Helen Keller was a prodigy of smelling. "The sense of smell," she wrote, "has told me of a coming storm hours before there was any sign of it visible. I notice first a throb of expectancy, a slight quiver, a concentration in my nostrils. As the storm draws near my nostrils dilate, the better to receive the flood of earth odors which seem to multiply and extend, until I feel the splash of rain against my cheek." Helen Keller and many others have testified that when a sense vanishes, those that remain do what they can to fill the breach.

Nonetheless, with each limitation of our senses, we come nearer death. The loss of seeing, hearing, touching, smelling, and tasting sentences us to insensate darkness, an isolation so complete that we can, without exaggeration, consider it a living death. Because every diminishment of our senses is a step in that direction, we fear it and fight against it.

Gratitude for What Remains

I'm tempted to say that when these limitations begin to manifest themselves, we gain excuses for failing to relate to the world in a proper way. This is particularly true for sight and hearing. If I don't see a problem, I can hardly be held responsible for it. If I don't hear instructions, I can hardly be blamed for not obeying them. Most husbands try this, though their eyesight may be as sharp as an eagle's and their hearing as acute as a bat's. But my wife would want me to mention the difference between not seeing and not noticing, as well as the difference between not hearing and not listening. I'm especially guilty of the latter, or so she keeps telling me. I maintain that my hearing isn't as good as it once was, but she's not convinced; she thinks I'm not paying close enough attention. That is why I won't refer to these excuses as a consolation. Most of us have had plenty of time to pay attention before our senses diminish, and those who want to pay attention find a way to do so, even with these limitations.

I'm also tempted to say that the limitations of our senses offer the consolation of not having to encounter some ugliness. With diminished senses, you wouldn't have to smell smoke or taste corked wine or feel a rash or hear rap or see an accident. You would be spared unpleasantness, to be sure, but that's just another way of saying you'd be spared participation in life. The way it works: the bad goes with the good, the ugly with the beautiful. You can't have one without the other. Most of us, I'm sure, would rather taste vinegar occasionally if that were the price of enjoying cabernet sauvignon. We would rather drink life to the full. So neither will I offer this as a consolation.

A more worthy one to consider, it seems to me, is that with every limitation of the senses, you can gain a more sincere gratitude for what remains. Sometimes you have to lose something—or at least begin to lose it—before you realize how wonderful it is.

Sarah Ban Breathnach was eating in a restaurant in the mid-1980s. A large ceiling panel suddenly fell on her, knocking her to the table. She didn't lose consciousness but sustained a head injury that left her bedridden for months and partially disabled for a year and a half. All her senses were skewed. Her eyesight was blurry and her eyes were so sensitive to light that the shades in her bedroom had to be permanently drawn. She couldn't listen to music, couldn't taste food, and couldn't smell her daughter's newly washed hair. The slightest touch on her skin was painful. These losses isolated her from others, even caused shame. In anguish she cried out to God, "Why me, why this, why now?" She discovered that sometimes God can be found in very unlikely places, such as a pot of spaghetti sauce.

As the aroma of a friend's kind gift simmering on the stove wafted up to my bedroom, I could scarcely believe my nose. Euphoric, I followed the strange but familiar fragrance of garlic,

169

onions, tomatoes, peppers and oregano down the stairs and into the kitchen. I was practically beside myself with delight. I felt like I was standing on holy ground in my own house. I had discovered the miracle of the sacred in the ordinary; from that moment my life would forever be changed.

Taking a spoon, I dipped it into the sauce and brought it to my lips. I wasn't able to taste the sauce yet, just distinguish temperature and texture. It didn't matter. I was so grateful to inhale the glorious scent of ordinary life that I was off and running. I went up to the bathroom and got out a jar of Vicks Vapo-Rub. *Yes! Eucalyptus!* Then I buried my face in some freshly laundered clothes and inhaled the fragrance of a warm shirt. And so it went.

For the next few happy weeks I rediscovered life with the same sense of wonder as my little girl. Taste came next, followed by hearing, sight and touch. Each sensory restoration was accompanied by a feeling of rapture and even sudden tears. Biting into a ripe, juicy peach. Listening to music. Seeing bright sunlight stream through a window. Being able to wear my favorite sweater. And, naturally, cradling my daughter in my arms again.

I was astonished and ashamed at my appalling lack of appreciation for what had been right under my nose. Cliché or not, we just don't know how blessed we are until misfortune strikes. No more. I swore I would never, ever forget.

Any diminishment of our senses reminds us that one way or another, through injury or illness or aging or death, we will experience their limitations, and this can be an encouragement to appreciate them to the fullest. I try to remind myself of this. When I'm hiking in the hills by our home, I think about each sense and what it's experiencing: my eyes see manzanita trees and the rocky hills of north San Diego County; my ears hear mockingbirds and wonderful silence; my tongue tastes a chocolate bar and the quench of water; my skin feels the shady cool of valleys and the intense heat of ridges; my nose smells pungent sage and my own sweat. I linger over each of these for many minutes, savoring it, and I ask God to grant me a truly grateful heart. The inevitable limitations of our senses alert us to a stark fact: none of them *have* to be; they are all gifts to be received with wonder and thanksgiving.

Another Realm

As we encounter the limitations of our senses, we may well discover another consolation: the diminishment of the world around us can encourage growth of the world within us. Though these limitations bring us nearer death, they teach us something we will one day experience in full: even in death, there is life. Darkness cannot dim what we see with an inner eye, nor can quietness dull what we hear with an inner ear. The death of our senses, and thus the passing of external distractions (both good and bad), might make possible the renewal of our spirits.

John Milton went blind, but when he was no longer able to see the physical world he saw with penetrating clarity the spiritual world. In 1667, peering deeply into the darkness, he penned the greatest epic in the English language, *Paradise Lost.* He followed this with *Paradise Regained* and *Samson Agonistes* in 1671.

Ludwig van Beethoven suffered the onset of deafness in 1801, and it worsened progressively until he was totally deaf by 1817. With no other sounds to distract him, he heard the music of his soul. At this time he wrote his works of greatest depth—the monumental Ninth Symphony, the *Missa Solemnis,* and his last five string quartets. When today, with our ears, we hear a choir sing his Ode to Joy, can we doubt that Beethoven, in his deafness, heard a music inaccessible to human ears, a music from outside his body or maybe deep within his body, a music that had its origin in another sphere?

171

It is theoretically possible, I suppose, that Milton could have written *Paradise Lost* had he not become blind, and Beethoven could have written the Ninth Symphony had he not become deaf. But I doubt it would have happened. The loss of their senses opened up something I do not believe would otherwise have been accessible to them.

The limitations of our senses tell us that we are more than bodies—and that *more*, we might discover, flows out of an uncreated light, an eternal music, the fragrance of heaven, the delights of the kingdom's banquet table, the warmth of God's embrace.

18

The Relentless, Inexorable, and Maddening Tick of the Clock

The Limitations of Time

Last Christmas, to be a good husband, I accompanied my wife to the mall to shop for presents. After what felt like a very long day I said, "Well, I think we've been pretty productive," which was my way of saying, "I think it's time to go home." I said this cheerfully because my mood always lifts when I'm about to receive a well-deserved pat on the back for being a good sport.

"What do you mean?" Shari said. "We can't leave yet. We've only been here an hour!"

"Are you sure?"

"Yes, we got here at 3:00. It's now 4:00."

That was a technical detail, in my judgment. For me, time spent shopping passes at exactly the same pace as when I'm having a root canal. On the other hand, I can spend a whole day sailing, photographing, or hiking, and it will seem no more than an hour; late in the afternoon it will occur to me that I've forgotten to eat lunch, noon having come and gone without my noticing.

Time only seems to change speed, of course. Sixty equal seconds always make a minute; sixty equal minutes always make an hour; twenty-four equal hours always make a day. But my feelings about shopping differ so radically from my feelings about sailing that it seems, in one case, as if the minutes are pushing themselves in a wheelchair down the hallway of a convalescent home, whereas, in the other, they've put on their Nikes and are sprinting for Olympic gold. Our attitude toward what we're doing *in* time determines how we view the passing *of* time.

Wasting Time

But what is our attitude toward time itself? Apart from what we are doing with it, how do we feel about it?

Thornton Wilder's play *Our Town* portrays a strong sense of continuity and community. George and Emily grow up in Grover's Corners, New Hampshire, fall in love, and get married. But familiar routines can't protect them from dark tragedy. Emily dies in childbirth. After dying she learns she can return to relive one day in her life. Against the advice of those already buried in the cemetery, she chooses to go back for her twelfth birthday. She sees the hustle and bustle, the baking of the birthday cake, the wrapping of presents, and family members living in the same house but hardly noticing one another. Finally, in desperation, she cries out, "Oh Mama, just look at me one minute as though you really saw me. . . . Just for a moment now we're all together. Mama, just for a moment we're happy. *Let's look at one another.*" As Emily is led back to the cemetery, she

174

hears Simon Stimson, the organist and town drunk, say, "Yes, now you know. Now you know! That's what it was to be alive. To move about in a cloud of ignorance; to go up and down trampling on the feelings of those . . . of those about you. To spend and waste time as though you had a million years."

We are often blind to time's passing. We carry on with things, too busy to be aware of time's swift movement. We spend and waste it as though we had a million years.

Think of how much time we dedicate to a future that never seems to arrive. When I look back over my life, I'm saddened by how much of my energy and thoughts were spent longing for the arrival of something new. I looked forward to professional opportunities, but, when they came, I looked forward to bigger and better ones. I looked forward to Christmas, but before we sat under the tree to open presents, I looked forward to getting back to my usual routine. I looked forward to vacations, but when I should have been enjoying them, I looked forward to returning to work. You've probably felt similar things. Something seems embedded in our nature that orients us toward the future, that makes us long for time's passing as though we were not speeding swiftly to the end of it.

Managing Time

Perhaps we treat time's passing so cavalierly because, at an unconscious level, we actually dread its passing, just as we might whistle a happy tune aggressively to hide our fear of approaching footsteps on a dark night. Our behavior does seem oddly conflicted. We squander time and eagerly await its passing into the future, but we also do our best to protect it, manage it, and maximize it. We scribble instructions in Daytimers and punch in commands on Palm Pilots. We take "time management" seminars. We read books about how to organize ourselves into amazing productivity. We run ourselves ragged trying to cram every day with as much activity as possible. Perhaps we do these things because we have not been able to suppress fully a deep terror of time's relentless race toward extinction.

A few months ago, when we went off Daylight Savings Time, I lined up four watches on my desk to reset them as accurately as possible, down to the precise second. I intended to set one watch, then use it as a master for the others. As its second hand landed on twelve, I stopped it by pulling out the stem. I paused about thirty seconds, then telephoned the authority: "Good morning," she said, "at the tone, Pacific Standard Time will be nine fifty-nine and fifty seconds. *Beep.*" I steadied my thumb, waiting. "Good morning. At the tone, Pacific Standard Time will be ten o'clock, exactly. *Beep.*" I quickly pushed in the stem. Did I do it right? I kept listening. "Good morning. At the tone, Pacific Standard Time will be ten o'clock and ten seconds. *Beep.*" Yes! I now had one completely accurate watch.

As I was working on the others, it occurred to me that my efforts were actually a colossal waste of time. I am a writer. My need for a watch, on a scale of one to ten, is minus five. My workday starts when I make the commute down the hallway to my study; it ends when I have enough sentences. I need to know the time only when my wife and I go to church (I was once a pastor who developed a distinctly unchristian attitude toward chronic latecomers), when we go to a movie, and when I have an appointment to get my hair cut. Otherwise, the sun's position in the sky is about all I need to know.

My obsession with measuring time, I suspect, has to do with my increasing awareness of its passing. I now have more years behind me than in front of me. Every rotation of the second hand tells me that death is one minute closer. So perhaps my way of dealing with this, my way of carrying on despite the advancing threat, is to fiddle with my watches, almost like fetishes, and write in my Daytimer and set goals and make lists, as if by organizing myself into maximum efficiency I will somehow

176

lock the door against the unwelcome visitor whose footsteps I already hear on the porch.

We may be conflicted about time, but this is certain: time will not wait for us to resolve these conflicts. The clock will keep ticking.

Savoring Now

The first consolation this confers is encouragement to live in the present. If you delete from your thoughts everything related to the past or the future, how much will actually be left? Very little, no doubt. Most of us are constantly bifurcated between yesterday's painful regrets and happy memories and tomorrow's anxious worries and eager expectancies. But, strictly speaking, the past and future are only abstract concepts—times that never *are*. All that really exists is the present. When do we pause long enough to enter its reality, to receive its gifts? When do we allow ourselves to *be* in what *is?*

This morning, after a cup of coffee and an attempt at meditation, I went outside to get the newspaper. As usual, I was a man on a mission, not wanting to waste any time because I needed to get to my desk and send an article to an editor and finish this chapter. Then—and I was already imagining this (it was in the future)—I would relax with my wife and friends at an Italian restaurant and enjoy myself, though what will likely happen, I know, is that while I'm eating pasta, I'll be looking forward to returning home so I can crawl into bed and read a novel, which will not be nearly as pleasurable as I expect because one of my eyes will keep shutting, first the left and then the right, until they find each other's rhythm and both close and the book drops. I wasn't thinking about these things as I picked up the newspaper. I was in my usual hurry, as I said, but something suddenly edged its way into the corner of my eye: the eastern sky had been sun-splashed with vermilion and orange. The drama of it jerked my head up, and for a moment I even forgot about the newspaper. Gashes of brilliant color spread across the sky, most intense in the east and reaching as far as the western hills. Standing there, I noticed something else: a powerful aroma of some sort. What was it? The little white flowers on the bush? How long had they been there? Perhaps because I had been thinking about this chapter, it occurred to me that I should enter that moment, suck all the pleasure out of it, savor it fully. I wondered, *How many more perfect mornings will there be in my life?* There was nothing morbid about this. I was simply aware that my mornings were passing and that I had better not wait until a vacation or retirement before pausing to enjoy them. There would always be a future filled with work and worry. But when would *now* receive its due? When would I enter fully into the only place where I really lived, the present?

The relentless, inexorable, and maddening tick of the clock says, "Make each tick count!" Pay attention to the present. Be open and attentive to what's happening—the smell of the pages of the book in your hands, the languid liquidity of your body in an easy chair, the sound of your kids in the other room, the smell of supper in the oven, the warm cup of tea, the tick of the clock on the wall. Take whatever this precise moment offers; consume it greedily with thanksgiving. Even if you live to be a hundred years old, you won't have too many of them left.

Letting Death Out of the Basement

The limitations of time grant another gift. It is a "consolation," though some effort may be necessary to understand why. None of the limitations of life so forcefully confronts us with the limitations of life itself. The ticking of the clock speaks loudly of the terror we most fear, the terror that puts the sting in all limitations—death.

178

Several times in this book I have referred to Ernest Becker's insightful book *The Denial of Death*. He shows how we construct our lives around patterns of denial; we create characters and assume neuroses that will help shield us from the dreadful reality of our demise. Part of our unconscious strategy in this endeavor is to transfer our hopes for salvation to others, turning them into stand-in heroes to help us gain immortality. This is not a conscious plan, but it is certainly real, and we must conclude that death is not simply something in our future. It is a present reality, a part of *now*.

Time's passing brings death up from the cellar of our consciousness, where it usually resides, and demands that we look at it. It blocks all our usual escape routes. The ticking of the clock says, "You can run but you can't hide, not forever. You are going to die. Face it. Deal with it."

The consoling aspect of this may not be readily evident. The next couple of chapters will, I hope, amplify the blessings of this terrifying encounter. For now, let me put it starkly: to grow into the full measure of our humanity, we must acknowledge and accept our mortality. We will never find salvation from our terror through denial; we will never escape our deepest fear by running and hiding and lying to ourselves. How could we? Any ruse can never do more than keep death buried in our unconscious, and there, hidden from sight, it does its worst work. From within the dark corners of the basement, death whispers its threats through the ductwork of our being and so causes us frantically to build and remodel the structure of our lives, boarding up old rooms and adding on new rooms, sawing and nailing and painting, keeping ourselves busy enough to pretend we don't hear the chill whispers of our mortality. If there is salvation from this terror, it will come only through letting death out of the basement and confronting it in the light of conscious awareness. We will not—cannot—defeat this foe by running from it.

Ernest Becker, at the end of his book, struggles to find some way to live in the presence of death, some way to go forward honestly and courageously. He is not altogether successful, in my judgment. But in the final passages he offers this wisdom:

> I think that taking life seriously means something such as this: that whatever man does on this planet has to be done in the lived truth of the terror of creation, of the grotesque, of the rumble of panic underneath everything. Otherwise it is false. Whatever is achieved must be achieved from within the subjective energies of creatures, without deadening, with the full exercise of passion, of vision, of pain, of fear, and of sorrow. How do we know—with Rilke—that our part of the meaning of the universe might not be a rhythm of sorrow?

Whatever we do, Becker tells us, we must live honestly, acknowledging "the rumble of panic underneath everything." That is where we must start. So far as we are able, we must face the harsh realities of life—all its limitations and, most of all, its end. This is frightening, to say the least. It might lead us into the rhythm of sorrow, but if this, too, is part of the meaning of the universe, what choice do we have?

Anticipating Eternity

Becker offers little more than an admonition to carry on despite the knowledge of mortality, in part because he is too honest for easy bromides. One of the most popular, he knows, is religion, which may simply be another defense mechanism, a form of denial. Philip Larkin, writing of death's terror, says, "This is a special way of being afraid/ No trick dispels. Religion used to try, / That vast moth-eaten musical brocade/ Created to pretend we never die." Becker may not be this harsh, but he doesn't want liturgies and hymns to drown out the "rumble of panic under everything."

Nonetheless, we must ask an important question: What if our longing for eternity exists for two reasons, both because we are headed for a death that terrifies *and* because we have been created for an eternity that exists? To imagine life beyond time may be simply another denial. But if it is a reality, not to imagine it would be a worse denial, for we would destroy the hope that enables courage and, in the end, even saves.

I think the Stage Manager in *Our Town* speaks for most of us:

> Now there are some things we all know, but we don't take'm out and look at'm very often. We all know that something is eternal. And it ain't houses and it ain't names, and it ain't earth, and it ain't even the stars . . . everybody knows in their bones that something is eternal, and that something has to do with human beings. All the greatest people ever lived have been telling us that for five thousand years and yet you'd be surprised how people are always losing hold of it. There's something way down deep that's eternal about every human being.

If the Stage Manager is correct—and I believe he is—then the limitations of time render valuable service. They lift our eyes toward something beyond time; they make us look beyond the horizon of the temporal into the vastness of eternity. Time's passing, as we have seen, encourages us to seize the present, but it does more: it transforms our longing for the future into a longing for eternity. We could say it radicalizes anticipation. We have learned to distrust the promises of time; the future never really delivers, never really satisfies our longings. So we must cast the anchor of hope much farther, all the way into eternity.

19

It Won't Get Any Better
The Limitations of Optimism

To illustrate the advantage of an optimistic spirit, Zig Ziglar tells the story of General Creighton Abrams, who, finding himself completely surrounded by the enemy, attempted to rally his troops by saying, "Men, now, for the first time in the history of this campaign, we are in a position to attack the enemy in any direction!"

This story demonstrates the best of the American spirit. How you look at a situation makes all the difference, we like to think, so do your best to think positively about it. You may be down, but you're not out. Look at the part of the glass that's half full, not the part that's half empty. Just like the little train in the children's story, tell yourself, "I think I can, I think I can, I think I can," and you, too, will get to the other side of the mountain.

As I mentioned in the first chapter, we live in an optimistic culture. Positive thinking is in the air we breathe; it's oxygen for the bloodstream of our national life. Gloomy people are in our midst, of course; depression is a problem for almost everyone once in a while and for some of us much of the time. But overall, we're a can-do folk, firmly convinced that when the going gets tough, the tough get going, and we plan to be among the tough. We shall overcome someday, oh yes. Others may fail, but not us, no siree, we *shall* overcome, if not today then tomorrow, and if not tomorrow then someday.

But there are limitations in life! Throughout this book, we've been acknowledging that in every area of life we crash into walls—walls that cannot be leapt over, no matter how positively we think or how much effort we expend. This being the case, it should be obvious that there are limitations to optimism itself. A positive spirit can take us a long way; it provides immense help in slogging through thick discouragement and breaking beyond formidable barriers. We do well to cultivate this attitude, choosing, so far as we can, to believe in ourselves and other people and especially the future. But we should not be deceived: not *all* things are possible. Optimism, therefore, has only limited value. Sometimes it has no more worth than a deflated balloon, unable to get itself off the ground, let alone lift anything else.

Room for Pessimism

About twenty years ago, I wrote a book entitled *Waking from the American Dream*. In it I argued that disappointments are normal, even for the most positive of thinkers. The American dream tells us that with enough goodwill and hard work we will achieve personal fulfillment. This myth supplies much motivation, both personally and nationally. But eventually we must wake up. Life is hard, often unbearably so, and sometimes there is nothing we can do about it.

The book was published in the 1980s, when Ronald Reagan's cheerful optimism blanketed the culture. The last thing anyone wanted was to wake from the American dream. If I had written a book promising happiness and success, I would probably be retired by now. But I thought there might be a market for an honest acknowledgment of the dark side of human experience. I was wrong. There was no market for this, at least for the way I presented it. But I was pleased that the half dozen or so people who read it said, in so many words, "You know, I've been working so hard, trying my best to have the proper attitude and to do the right things, and frankly, I'm tired. It's a relief to hear someone say that disappointment is part of being human."

That relief is the first consolation of the limitations of optimism. It's oddly comforting to know that you don't have to be sunny all the time. It takes energy—sometimes a great deal of energy—to be relentlessly and cheerfully expectant. It's not easy to keep cranking up a positive spirit, especially after crashing against some walls that, instead of giving way to your determination, refuse to budge and leave you a crumpled heap. You might be able to get up and try it a few more times, but, eventually, you get worn out.

Acknowledging the limitations of optimism means making room for pessimism. Sometimes pessimism is entirely appropriate, a reasonable response, an honest dedication to reality. G. K. Chesterton wrote that "pessimism is not always inane and drifting . . . pessimism is sometimes courageous; strange as it may seem, it is sometimes cheerful." To name some truths takes boldness, but from that naming comes a kind of satisfaction. This is not unlike the pleasure provided by fairy tales, in which our darkest fears are embodied in wicked witches and dangerous dragons, and, thus named, are more easily confronted.

In my work as a pastor, I often saw individuals who were dying of cancer or some other disease trying hard to "keep the faith," doing their best to believe they would be healed, struggling to keep every thought positive even as death tightened its grim grip. Neither family members nor friends would want to undermine this optimism, of course, so they would dance around the painful truth, pretending not to see it, with the consequence that everyone was left to suffer in lonely solitude.

Then I would express the truth as matter-of-factly as possible; I would say something like, "Though we keep praying for God's healing, and though we believe anything is possible, your disease appears to be getting worse and you will likely experience death before the rest of us." More often than not, a visible relief swept over them. They felt liberated, I think, from having to be optimistic. Honest pessimism about their chances of survival conferred two necessary freedoms: freedom for the inner work of coming to terms with death, and freedom for the outer work of honest conversations with others—conversations of healing, with memories shared and forgiveness granted and love expressed.

Surrendering to Death

I have used the above example of dying for a reason. The limitations of optimism lead to something more than pessimism. Stated bluntly, they lead to death. All the limitations we have considered in this book compel us to see the limitations of optimism, and this knowledge pries open an inner door, from which escapes an awareness of the limitation we fear most, *the* limitation—death. We have spent much of our lives building defenses against this enemy, sometimes consciously but more often unconsciously, and now we are completely defenseless.

There is nothing left but surrender.

Once again, the consolation in this might not be readily evident. But it's the second greatest consolation we will ever receive, because it makes possible the greatest of all consolations—resurrection. It's tempting to rush straight to the good news of this renewal, but we're not yet ready for that. There is a definite order, not just in thinking but in *being*. We cannot experience the limitation of all limitations until the darkest of all has had its way with us. We cannot attain resurrection without death.

This, at any rate, is a core conviction of Christian faith. In Jesus Christ an astonishing reversal takes place. Much of what drives us, as the first chapters of Genesis teach, is a desire to take God's place, an arrogant striving to seize control, to rise above the limitations of our humanity. The Bible calls this sin. Contrary to what you might have been told, God's preferred way of dealing with this problem is not to blast sinners into the fires of hell but to lift them into the joys of new life. To accomplish this, God chose to do something so remarkable, so utterly unthinkable, you'd have to be God to come up with it: in Jesus Christ, God cancelled our arrogance with a supreme act of humility. Whereas we have been doing our best to become like God, God chose to become human; whereas we have been reaching upward, God chose to bend downward; whereas we have been fighting against all limitations, God chose the most severe limitation; whereas we have been striving for self-fulfillment, God chose self-emptying; whereas we have been running for dear life, God chose death.

Now Jesus Christ says, "Take up your own cross and follow me." This will be the scariest thing we've ever heard, because it asks us to reverse directions, to change the trajectory of our lives, to head toward what we fear most. But it will also be the best thing we've ever heard, because the invitation comes from the *Living* One, from the One who addresses us from the far side of the cross. "Trust me," he says. "The death you fear will lead into the life you were created to enjoy."

This is not, I must make clear, an invitation to suicide but to surrender. There is an immense difference. Suicide is the pursuit of death, the attempt to take death into our own hands, and it is, in a paradoxical way, simply another effort to escape the pain of limitations. The surrender we're called to is far more radical;

186

it is a release of our control, an acceptance of life *and all its limitations,* a falling, not happily but willingly, into something too dark to see but what we fear may be Nothing.

There is only one way to do this, I believe: trusting the One who speaks to us from the far side of death. At the end of optimism, we can find hope—hope in something far more than what we see, hope in life beyond the death we now know we cannot avoid.

Peace in the Tomb

During the darkest days of my life, when my past seemed ruined by failure and my future seemed nonexistent, when I could neither go backward to memories nor go forward to expectations, I rediscovered a story from the New Testament—the account of Jesus raising Lazarus from the dead in the eleventh chapter of the Gospel of John. I had read this story many, many times, even preached sermons on it. But my difficult circumstances enabled me to hear it afresh, and whereas I had always considered it a story about resurrection, I began to understand that it was as much about death.

The image I couldn't get out of my mind, the image I not only saw but somehow *felt* in the depths of my being, was the part I had always skipped over before, Lazarus lying in the tomb. Before he died, his sisters had asked Jesus for help. "Come quickly," they said, "for your friend Lazarus is ill." But Jesus, for some reason, didn't move, didn't even make an effort to help his friend. This part of the story seemed very true to me, for I had more than a few of my own spiritual disappointments. I, too, had asked for help as my world crumbled around me, but Jesus didn't seem to show up.

And now I was dead. My life was over. That may sound overly dramatic; in retrospect, it was an exaggeration, but at the time, it seemed as though I had died, been buried, and was lying in a cold tomb. I was Lazarus on a stone slab. He had lain there four days, but four days or four thousand, what difference did it make? Dead is dead. Lazarus had no hope, because hope presupposes enough life to look beyond the present.

I realized that I had nothing left to do. The only "work" required of me was the anti-work of surrender. I had wanted to be somebody, to achieve, to make a difference, to be successful in my relationships and my profession, to be a moral and spiritual man, but I had come to the limitations of all these, and they felt like the final limitation of death itself. Now there was nothing left but Nothing. Now I could only give in to the brokenness, the weakness, the impotence. I was Lazarus.

When I tried to pray or meditate, I imagined myself in the tomb. I felt the coldness, the stone beneath me, the emptiness and the darkness around me. I thanked God for the good that had been in my life, and I asked God to care for my loved ones—as though I were lost and gone forever.

But I wasn't quite dead. There was still a spark of ambition in me, still enough life to want to achieve. I wanted to be a good Lazarus. This sounds absurd, I know, but there is no other way of saying it: I wanted to be a good corpse. I wanted to be dead in the best possible way. So what should I do? Lazarus would be my model, but he wasn't much help because he just seemed to lie there in silence.

Then it occurred to me that that was precisely the point. A dead man does nothing. *Nothing!* The dead do not read self-help books and attend workshops on finding ways out of the grave; the dead do not improve their prayer life or follow disciplines of meditation; the dead do not join therapy groups or practice yoga or write in journals. The dead are in a state of *absolute* helplessness, complete surrender. When Lazarus lay in the grave, he did nothing but stink.

I wanted to believe there was something I could do while lying in the grave, some steps I could take, some disciplines to adopt, some methods to master. But this was like a chicken's body frantically running around after having its head cut off, the last stubborn attempt to salvage my life, to stay in control, which was actually the very thing that had to die.

So I let go, gave up, accepted that I was nothing but Lazarus. And this is what I discovered: accepting nothing-to-do is not as bad as it might seem. In fact, it's quite liberating. Lazarus is nothing if not relaxed, at peace.

Yes, Lazarus was wholly at peace, which is another way of saying absolutely dependent on grace. If resurrection would ever happen for him, it would only happen to him. The dead do not raise themselves; they are raised. We can speak of it only in the passive voice. Resurrection is not self-renewal, not the glorious conclusion of a program of self-improvement. It is a gift that comes from the outside. It is the grace of new creation. With nothing left to do but trust this grace, peace comes.

The Way to Life

We should not limit our view of death to the cessation of physical life, though that is its ultimate manifestation. Death is an event for more than our bodies. It can take place in our emotions, our worldview, our self-image, our sense of security. It is the pouring out of some part of ourselves into nothingness, the coming apart of what once was, the "dark night of the soul." It is an irrevocable loss, and thus unspeakably painful. This pain, moreover, is amplified because it heralds the final loss that terrifies us.

But the great paradox of our existence is that death leads to life. We shall consider this more fully in the next chapter, but it's important now to stress that *death* leads to life. Dante's *Divine Comedy* represents vividly what I'm trying to convey in this chapter: to reach heaven, we must descend into hell; the way up is the way down.

189

A Zen master once said that we should do our dying early so we can get on with the rest of our lives. He was expressing a sentiment at the heart of Christianity. Jesus said that whoever clings to life will lose it, but whoever loses life will gain it, and he sealed the truth of this by his own self-surrender unto death.

So the consolation when optimism dies is the encouragement to surrender to all life's limitations, to accept them as an inevitable part of being human, to see them as an opportunity to die and thus find life. Without optimism, we're left, finally, with the darkness of the tomb. That's a frightening prospect, to be sure. But Jesus Christ says, "Follow me," and Lazarus says, "It's more peaceful than you can imagine," and I say to you, give up and be a good corpse and you will discover that you're held not by a cold stone but by the arms of grace.

20

Finally, the Best News
The Limitation of Limitations

U nbind him, and let him go!"
These words were the first Lazarus heard through resin-hardened cloths. The voice was loud, filled with authority. Then he heard silence—the silence of a crowd too stunned to gasp or scream, the silence of tongue-tied bewilderment, the silence of awe not sure what to do with itself.

That's what he heard, and he was conscious of hearing it. Just as he was conscious of wondering whether anyone would have the courage to cut him out of the grave clothes, and conscious that he had just walked out of a cave in response to a command that had somehow *done* the thing it asked, and conscious that from a place very near where he had heard the command a laughter was rising, raucous and riotous, that would likely erupt in a manner less dignified than the occasion warranted. Not that it mattered. The crowd would think it mattered, though, because God knows they worried about everything.

He had been one of them once (an eternity ago), living on their side of the grave, flinching toward a terrifying future.

He had been sick and sought healing, even prayed. Then he died and didn't do much of anything, including pray. He was a model corpse. But now he was standing on his own two feet. The worst had happened, and he had lived through it, or, to be more accurate if more confusing, the best had happened, and it had lived through him. That's about all he could have told you at the moment: something had lived through him; a power outside of him had lifted him from the cold stone and out of nothingness into new life. Don't ask him to explain it, not yet. Maybe later he would understand more.

He had once been terrified. He had been living toward death, and that meant living toward what he had thought was his doom. Then he had fallen directly into that doom, sunk to the bottom of it, and there was such a thick finality about it that he didn't bother to flounder and flail but instead relaxed and found himself floating on it. He still felt borne along by it, as though he would always be dead, or at least dying. If he had once been living to die, now he was dying to live. The death he would in a way never leave would be the place of his birth, the start of something deeper and fuller and more complete. That's what he could see even when he couldn't yet see through the grave clothes. So the first thing the crowd heard from him was the sound of a dead man laughing.

Killing the Author of Life

That's how I imagine it might have happened as Jesus raised Lazarus from death. When Jesus finally showed up, Lazarus's sister Martha couldn't resist a gentle rebuke. "Lord," she said, "if you had been here, my brother would not have died." But Jesus told her not to worry. "I am the resurrection and the life," he said. "Those who believe in me, even though they die, will live, and everyone who lives and believes in me will never die." Jesus proved this dramatically by commanding Lazarus—four days dead, bound in resin-soaked grave clothes, and lying in a burial cave—to get up and live. And he did exactly that, to the astonishment of everyone, most of all to Lazarus himself.

The authorities were more than astonished; they were terrified. Their power rested on sanctions, and sanctions always rely on the threat of limitations, the ultimate of which is death. But if this Jesus, who had already been in their sights as a troublemaker, could bring a person out of the tomb, temporal power had encountered its own limitation. "So from that day on they planned to put him to death."

The irony is impossible to miss: they sought to kill the One who said, "I am the resurrection and the life." And they succeeded! This could only have happened because Jesus surrendered himself, gave himself up to the limitation we all face and fear. He did this, according to the Bible, to take upon himself the death we deserve for our willful separation from the Creator of life.

But death could not hold him. What turned a scattered group of disillusioned disciples into a band of martyrs and changed history forever was this: God raised Jesus from death. This confirmed that God had indeed been present in Jesus of Nazareth. The Author of Life had nails pounded into his hands and feet, and had a spear thrust into his side, and had thorns pressed on his brow; the Author of Life had cried out in despair and said, "It is finished!" But death's victory was only apparent. What was really finished was death. The resurrection of Jesus was a declaration that humanity's most terrifying limitation was now limited, that eternal life would triumph.

As those first followers of Jesus huddled at the foot of the cross, they could not imagine the new order of existence that was about to burst upon them. Their master seemed no match for the limitation that threatened them all—a limitation that had uttered its final, mocking taunt against all human aspirations. But then, resurrection! At first, they couldn't believe it; it was too good to be true. Then they came to understand that it was too good not to be true. It showed that "in Christ God was reconciling the world to himself."

Thus the crucifixion of Jesus, of all humanity's shameful acts the most evil, was used by God for good purposes. God turned Black Friday into Good Friday; God, in an act of staggering grace, took something wholly evil and transformed it into something wholly redemptive. Where hate unleashed its worst, love conquered with the best.

Resurrection Happens

I have ventured a summary of core Christian convictions because they are very much to the point of this book. If God was present in Jesus Christ, then the divine has entered the worst limitation we face—indeed, as we have seen, the one that terrifies us the most—and turned it inside out, refashioned it from within, transformed it from something evil into something redemptive. When death had done its worst (claiming the Author of Life), resurrection happened. This, in my judgment, is the only answer to the question that remains after Ernest Becker's analysis of our predicament. How shall we carry on with the knowledge of our dreadful end? *We shall carry on because resurrection happens.* The raising of Jesus supplies us with hope—and not simply hope that one day we, too, will live beyond the grave, but hope that every limitation, by the same grace of God, can be transformed into something more, something healing and redemptive and life-giving. This is the ultimate consolation of every limitation.

We have every reason to believe, on the basis of what happened to Jesus, that God is able and more than willing to take limitations that at best annoy us and at worst fill us with dread and, in ways we cannot yet see or understand, make them serve the purposes of love. This does not make them less painful; this does not make them good in themselves. But it can make them easier to bear, knowing their No! will somehow be turned into a Yes!

194

The Last Laugh

So the consolation that comes with this final limitation—the limitation of limitations—is a revelation of a revolution, the unveiling of an upheaval. That which was once our enemy will be changed into a servant of our good. If God can succumb to *the* limitation—death—and transform it, by the strength of eternal love, into the world's salvation, if the cross can be converted from an ugly instrument of death into an adored object of inspiration, then we can move beyond optimism into an assured hope that our own death will become a doorway into life, a translation into an order of being that we cannot now comprehend. This being the case, we have good reason to believe that all the other limitations, while difficult and often painful, will also become, in the hands of God, instruments of healing and growth that will finally make possible the fulfillment of joy.

God has the last laugh, in other words. There is an ancient Russian Orthodox tradition that devotes the day after Easter to sitting around a table and telling jokes. Why? According to William J. Bausch,

> this was the way, they felt, that they were imitating that cosmic joke that God pulled on Satan in the resurrection. Satan thought he had won, and was smug in his victory, smiling to himself, having had the last word. So he thought. Then God raised Jesus from the dead, and life and salvation became the last words. And the whole world laughed at the devil's discomfort. This attitude passed into the medieval concept of *hilaritas*, which did not mean mindless giggling, but that even at the moment of disaster one may wink because he or she knows there is a God.

The limitations of life, by themselves, are no joke. There is nothing funny about bodies wearing out, relationships coming to grief, achievements falling short, money running out, time slipping away, or any of the others. But when we view these things in the light of Easter, we must wink, if not laugh. We know that the story is not yet finished; if it now seems like a tragedy, it will, by an astonishing turn of events, become a comedy.

Eugene O'Neill, in his play *Lazarus Laughed,* imagined the newly raised man having a conversation with the Roman Caligula. Describing himself in the tomb, Lazarus says,

> In the dark peace of the grave the man Lazarus rested. He was still weak, as one who recovers from a long illness—for, living, he had believed his life a sad one! [*He laughs softly, and softly they all echo his laughter.*] He lay dreaming to the croon of silence, feeling as the flow of blood in his own veins the past reenter the heart of God to be renewed by faith into the future. He thought: "Men call this death"—for he had been dead only a little while and he still remembered. Then, of a sudden, a strange gay laughter trembled from his heart as though his life, so long repressed in him by fear, had found at last its voice and a song for singing.

Our lives have long been repressed by fear of the limitations we must suffer. But whereas we, through strategies of self-survival, have denied death, God, through a strategy of self-sacrifice, has defeated death. This triumph of life means that we, too, can find our voices and our songs for singing.

Notes

Chapter 1

12 "There is *nothing* . . . about in boats." Kenneth Grahame, *The Wind in the Willows* (New York: Charles Scribner's Sons, 1960), p. 6.

14 "We resist the . . . for an answer." Parker Palmer, *Let Your Life Speak: Listening for the Voice of Vocation* (San Francisco: Jossey-Bass, 2000), p. 39.

15 We're doing our . . . pretensions to happiness. William James, *Varieties of Religious Experience—A Study in Human Nature* (New York: New American Library, 1958), p. 121.

16 "Not once in . . . like a dream." Walker Percy, *The Second Coming* (New York: Farrar, Straus, and Giroux, 1980), pp. 123–24.

17 "consists in my . . . constraint diminishes strength." As quoted in Fred Craddock, *As One without Authority* (St. Louis: Chalice, 2001), p. 101.

Chapter 2

22 the average age . . . "end of youth" is fifty-four. "Vital Statistics," *Health*, January/February 2000, p. 22.

22 the number of . . . amount in 1992. From www.plasticsurgery.org.

23 "are *the* official . . . 1990s, you know." As quoted in Karen Lee-Thorp and Cynthia Hicks, *Why Beauty Matters* (Colorado Springs: Navpress, 1997), p. 149.

23 "No one knows . . . a thousand websites." Elizabeth Pope, "51 Top Scientists Blast Anti-Aging Idea," *AARP Bulletin,* June 2002, p. 7.

27 "The ten years . . . a lucky man." Michael J. Fox, *Lucky Man* (New York: Hyperion, 2002), p. 5.

28 "To view human . . . off to war." Andre Dubus, *Meditations from a Movable Chair* (New York: Knopf, 1998), p. 155.

28 "Living in the world . . . voice embraced me." Andre Dubus, *Broken Vessels* (Boston: David R. Godine, 1991), pp. 143–44.

Chapter 3

32 Another study of . . . other negative factors. Claudia Wallis, "Stress: Can We Cope?" *Time* (6 January 1983), p. 48, as quoted in William E. Hulme, *Managing Stress in Ministry* (San Francisco: Harper and Row, 1985), p. 25.

33 The joint, as . . . one of them. As quoted in Robert Raines, *Creative Brooding* (New York: Macmillian, 1966), p. 48.

35 an uncle who, . . . for forty years. Mary Karr, *The Liars' Club* (New York: Viking, 1995).

37 *taming of terror.* . . . and combat them. Ernest Becker, *The Denial of Death* (New York: Free Press, 1997), p. 145.

38 then he experiences . . . dependencies and emotions. Ibid., p. 146.

38 "universal phenomenon . . . the human mind." Ibid.

41 To learn to love. . . wholly within love. Madeleine L'Engle, *Lines Scribbled on an Envelope* (New York: Farrar, Straus, and Giroux, 1969), p. 49. Used by permission.

Chapter 4

46 Carl Sandburg wrote . . . Carnegie Hall at eighty-nine. John E. Biegert, *So We're Growing Older* (New York: Pilgrim, 1982), p. 13.

48 "for God knows . . . good and evil." Genesis 3:4.

Chapter 5

56 we may still . . . may call self-actualization. Abraham H. Maslow, *Motivation and Personality* (New York: Harper and Row, 1954), p. 46.

56 "Because I have . . . am making progress." As quoted in Karl Barth, *A Late Friendship—The Letters of Karl Barth and Carl Zuckmayer* (Grand Rapids: Eerdmans, 1983), p. 21.

56 "All people in . . . esteem of others." Abraham H. Maslow, *Motivation and Personality* (New York: Harper and Row, 1954), p. 45.

59–60 Compromises I had . . . of a seminary. I tell more of this story in *The Wisdom of Pelicans—A Search for Healing at the Water's Edge* (New York: Viking, 2002).

62 "When my soul . . . my right hand." Psalm 73:21–23.

Chapter 6

66 It is what . . . are ashamed of." June Singer, *Boundaries of the Soul—The Practice of Jung's Psychology* (New York: Doubleday, 1972), p. 165.

69 The larger we . . . fulfilling our potential. For this image of two circles overlapping, I'm indebted to Robert Johnson, *Owning Your Own Shadow* (San Francisco: HarperSanFrancisco, 1991), pp. 95 ff.

70 "The woman was very beautiful." 2 Samuel 11:2.

71 "I have sinned against the Lord." 2 Samuel 12:13.

71 Have mercy on . . . ever before me." Psalms 51:1, 3.

72 One incident from . . . compassion and forgiveness. The story of David and Shimei is found in 2 Samuel 16: 5–14 and 19:16–23.

73 "Anyone who has . . . someone who hasn't." As quoted in *Bits and Pieces*, June 1987, p. 13.

Chapter 7

77–78 "There is an . . . in the mud." As quoted in "To Quote . . .," *Leadership*, spring 1997, p. 73.

78 "Blessed are the . . . kingdom of heaven." Matthew 5:3.

79 When others testify . . . under the pew. See my book *Finding Happiness in the Most Unlikely Places* (Downers Grove, Ill.: InterVarsity Press, 1990), pp. 29 ff.

80–81 Gideon is out . . . passion is unreasonable. Brennan Manning, *Lion and Lamb* (Old Tappan, N.J.: Chosen, 1986), pp. 96–97.

Chapter 8

82–83 "I love her, . . . the same bed?" A. J. Jacobs, "The Endorsement: Separate Beds," *Esquire*, September 2002, p. 80.

83 I have sought . . . poets have imagined. As quoted in Judith Viorst, *Necessary Losses* (New York: Simon and Schuster, 1986), p. 190.

84 "cannot distinguish itself . . . is no identity." M. Scott Peck, *The Road Less Traveled—A New Psychology of Love, Traditional Values and Spiritual Growth* (New York: Simon and Schuster, 1978), p. 85.

84 "When it is . . . its mother's command." Ibid.

84–85 The essence of . . . Loneliness is no more! Ibid., p 87.

86 Funny how I . . . someone's entire day. Philip Simmons, *Learning to Fall—The Blessings of an Imperfect Life* (New York: Bantam, 2000), pp. 69–70.

88 cones open most . . . and fallen trees. Morton Kelsey, *Reaching* (San Francisco: Harper and Row, 1989), pp. 85–86.

89 This love reveals . . . *of the beloved.* For this idea, I am indebted to Diogenes Allen, *Love—Christian Romance, Marriage, Friendship* (Cambridge: Cowley, 1987).

Chapter 9

92 Yesterday, in preparation . . . their spare time! Shere Hite, *The Hite Report on Male Sexuality* (New York: Knopf, 1981).

93 But consider this . . . a slow day. Sam Keen, *Fire in the Belly—On Being a Man* (New York: Bantam, 1991), p. 71.

94 "We are in flight . . . *passion of eros.*" Rollo May, *Love and Will* (New York: Norton, 1969), p. 65.

94 "What of the . . . *this new freedom?*" Ibid., p. 69.

94 "We go to bed . . . away one's head." Ibid., p. 71.

95 "an appealing symbolic . . . which he creates life." Ibid., p. 72.

95 Sex can be . . . and good life. Ibid., pp. 73–74.

96 The soul of . . . brought into the enterprise. Thomas Moore, *The Soul of Sex* (New York: HarperCollins, 1998), pp. 184–85.

Chapter 10

98 "I would have . . . theory is correct." Clifton Fadiman, ed., *The Little, Brown Book of Anecdotes* (Boston: Little, Brown, 1985), p. 186.

98 "The bigger they . . . harder they fall." Ibid., p. 209.

98–99 "I am willing . . . am never wrong." Ibid., p. 248.

106–107 The disciples of Jesus. . . the way down. Matthew 14:22–33.

107 "We were so . . . raises the dead." 2 Corinthians 1:8–9.

Chapter 11

111 When we receive . . . load of shame. C. W. Ellison, "Self-Esteem," *Baker Encyclopedia of Psychology*, ed., David G. Benner (Grand Rapids: Baker, 1985), pp. 1045–47.

111 "For everything there . . . matter under heaven." Ecclesiastes 3:1.

117 During my first . . . for my soul. *The Wisdom of Pelicans—A Search for Healing at the Water's Edge* (New York: Viking, 2002).

Chapter 12

123–124 "Our real problems . . . do not believe." As quoted in Karl Menninger, *Whatever Became of Sin?* (New York: Dutton, 1973), pp. 151–52.

124 In Victor Hugo's . . . him to his death. As retold by Bruce W. Theilemann, "The Cry of Mystery," *Preaching Today*, tape no. 66.

125 "Take care! . . . abundance of possessions." Luke 12:15.

125 He issued this . . . two fighting brothers. Luke 12:13–15.

126 "God said to . . . rich toward God." Luke 12:16–21.

Chapter 14

140–141   The only way . . . instead of life. Frederick Buechner, *Telling Secrets* (San Francisco: HarperSanFrancisco, 1991), pp. 26–27.

Chapter 15

152   "emptied himself . . . above every name." Philippians 2:7–9.

Chapter 16

155   "pleasure is labour . . . tires as much." William Cowper, as quoted in *The Oxford Dictionary of Quotations* (Oxford: Oxford University Press, 1979), p. 165.

155–156   A child kicks . . . a theatrical *encore*. G. K. Chesterton, *Orthodoxy* (New York: Image, 1959), p. 60.

160   "love, joy, peace, . . . gentleness, and self-control." Galatians 5:22.

160   "In my end is my beginning." T. S. Eliot, "East Coker," *The Complete Poems and Plays* (New York: Harcourt, Brace, and World, 1971), p. 129.

Chapter 17

163   "Smells detonate softly . . . of the undergrowth." Diane Ackerman, *A Natural History of the Senses* (New York: Random, 1990), p. 5.

165   an onrushing, cresting, . . . brain: We *hear*. Ibid., p. 177.

166   "The greatest thing . . . all in one." As quoted in ibid., p. 227.

168   "The sense of . . . against my cheek" As quoted in ibid., p. 44.

169–170   As the aroma . . . never, ever forget. Sarah Ban Breathnach, "Coming to My Senses," *Readers' Digest*, November 2002, p. 61.

Chapter 18

175   "Yes, now you . . . a million years." Thornton Wilder, *Our Town* (New York: Harper and Row, 1985), p. 101.

180 I think that . . . rhythm of sorrow? Ernest Becker, *The Denial of Death* (New York: Free Press, 1997), p. 284.

180 "This is a . . . we never die." Philip Larkin, "Aubade," *Collected Poems* (New York: Farrar, Straus, and Giroux, 1988), p. 208.

181 Now there are . . . every human being. Wilder, *Our Town*, p. 81.

Chapter 19

182 "Men, now, for . . . in any direction!" Zig Ziglar, *See You At The Top* (Gretna, La.: Pelican, 1975), p. 336.

184 "pessimism is not . . . is sometimes cheerful." G. K. Chesterton, *A Handful of Authors: Essays on Books and Writers* (New York: Sheed and Ward, 1953), p. 104.

Chapter 20

191 "Unbind him, and let him go." John 11:44.

192 "Lord, if you . . . not have died." Ibid. v. 21.

192 "I am the resurrection . . . will never die." Ibid. vv. 25–26.

193 "So from that . . . him to death." Ibid, v. 53.

194 "in Christ God . . . world to himself." 2 Corinthians 5:18.

195 this was the . . . is a God. William J. Bausch, *Storytelling —Imagination and Faith* (Mystic, Conn.: Twenty-Third Publications, 1984), p. 138.

196 In the dark . . . song for singing. Eugene O'Neill, *Lazarus Laughed* (New York: Boni & Liveright, 1927), p. 71.